Please Return to:
Rosie Peterson
760-443-6471

Bless
This
Child

*A Comprehensive
Guide to Creating Baby
Blessing Ceremonies*

REV. SUSANNA STEFANACHI MACOMB
with
ANDREA THOMPSON

iUniverse, Inc.
Bloomington

iUniverse books may be ordered through booksellers or by contacting:

iUniverse
1663 Liberty Drive
Bloomington, IN 47403
www.iuniverse.com
1-800-Authors (1-800-288-4677)

Because of the dynamic nature of the Internet, any Web addresses or links contained in this book may have changed since publication and may no longer be valid. The views expressed in this work are solely those of the author and do not necessarily reflect the views of the publisher, and the publisher hereby disclaims any responsibility for them.

Any people depicted in stock imagery provided by Thinkstock are models, and such images are being used for illustrative purposes only.

Certain stock imagery © Thinkstock.

ISBN: 978-1-4620-4973-8 (sc)
ISBN: 978-1-4620-4971-4 (hc)
ISBN: 978-1-4620-4972-1 (e)

Library of Congress Control Number: 2011915948

Printed in the United States of America

iUniverse rev. date: 11/4/2011

Dedicated to my son, Adam, and all the blessed children and their parents

Acknowledgments

I am inspired by the families that generously opened their hearts and shared their stories. It has been a privilege to walk beside your marriages, your births—your transformation. A joy! Thank you for your greatness of spirit.

I am so grateful for the magic of the children. They bring us back to purity, innocence and glee. There is so much God in them.

I especially want to thank my collaborator, Andrea Thompson. To quote scripture, *She is worth far more than rubies*. I am honored to call her friend, a sister.

Thank you to Elaine Zervos, my organizing angel and keeper of the calendar, for her unwavering faith and support. You are a gift.

Thank you to Fred Courtright, our permissions expert, for his help.

Three souls left the earth not long ago: the late Rabbi Joseph Gelberman, my spiritual and practical teacher and founder of the first interfaith seminary; the late Pir Vilayat Inayat Khan, the man who brought Sufism to America, who touched me on a mystical level; the late Very Reverend Forrest Church, former pastor of All Souls Unitarian Church in New York, where I have had the privilege of conducting ceremonies. These three lights each contributed to interfaith, intercultural peace. Thank you.

Finally, with tears in my eyes and a heart full of love, my thanks to my husband of 25 years, Edward, and my son, Adam, who will always be my beautiful, beautiful boy. None of this would be possible without you.

Contents

Preface xi

Introduction: About This Book xiii

PART I FIRST STEPS 1

  1. With Each Child, the World Begins Anew! 3

  2. Thinking about Your Ceremony:
     A Questionnaire for Parents 9

  3. Logistics: The Who, What, Where, and
     When of Your Baby Blessing Ceremony 17

  4. Sensitivities and Considerations for the Interfaith Family 25

PART II THE BABY BLESSING CEREMONY:
          A MENU OF ELEMENTS 33

  Readings, Prayers, Blessings, Rituals, and Quotes 34
  Processional 35
  Welcoming Words 35
  Readings 38
  Rituals 61

PART III MOTHERS, FATHERS, BABIES 83

  Real Life Stories, Real Life Ceremonies 84

PART IV DOWN THE YEARS 125

  Raising Your Child in Spiritual Wisdom 126

A Final Word 137

A Resource Directory 139

Permissions Acknowledgments 145

About the Author 147

Preface

When my first book, *Joining Hands and Hearts: Interfaith, Intercultural Celebrations, A Practical Guide for Couples*, was published, *Publishers Weekly* called it "cutting edge." It was the first of its kind. *Bless This Child* is also cutting edge. To my knowledge, this is the first book that deals in depth with the subject of creating personalized baby blessing ceremonies. It is also the first book that really addresses the needs of interfaith families wanting to combine their traditions, along with the various issues that arise.

Of all ceremonies, baby blessings are my favorite because of the babies themselves. The energy babies exude and bring forth from others is magical! People transform to their more innocent, gleeful selves around the youngest members of our society. So it is with great joy that we give you *Bless This Child*. May it help you create a ceremony that reflects the wonder and magic that is your child.

Introduction: About This Book

Every baby born is unique. An astonishing miracle. And when that son or daughter finally arrives, after the months of preparations and planning and anticipation, parents naturally want to gather family and friends for a joyous occasion. Even more than the birth day itself, a baby-naming ceremony celebrates new beginnings, the reconfiguration of the planets! This is a time parents say to their child:

- *We welcome you.*

- *We are beside ourselves with joy because you are here.*

- *We name you.*

- *We introduce you to the people you will come to know and who will know you, watch over you, and love you as we do.*

- *We share with all here today our promises and hopes for you for the years ahead.*

So many wish to express those sentiments in a one-of-a-kind ceremony, to celebrate their one-of-a-kind child. They want an unforgettable event that not only acknowledges the solemnity of the occasion, but that moves all gathered to moments of laughter and to happy tears.

Bless This Child is for those parents and their families.

Bless This Child is for the clergy and humanist officiants who conduct these ceremonies.

In this book, you will learn:

- how to arrange and design a personalized baby blessing ceremony, including who, what, when, and where suggestions;

- how to give a loving role to siblings, grandparents, and godparents;

- how to honor a mix of family religions, traditions, and cultures.

In this book, you will find:

- a lengthy menu of suggested readings, blessings, prayers, and quotes selected from the world's most eloquent and most eternal writings;

- elegant and heart-touching rituals that can be incorporated into any ceremony, here explained and fully scripted;

- tender counsel for the interfaith family, to help ensure that grandparents and others will feel comfortable and included;

- real-life stories and examples of ceremonies that demonstrate the many possibilities in design and content;

- a resource directory that will help you locate a celebrant and/or a chapel, arrange for baptismal and baby naming certificates or documents, and more.

In *Bless This Child*, you will find information that has not previously been gathered in any other one book or resource.

Consider this a workbook. Read through it, mark it up, dog-ear the pages if you want. You will see that in some sections blank spaces have been left for you to write directly onto the pages. I suggest that in the Menu section you take a pencil and circle your preferences. Use a pencil with an eraser, so you will be able to go back and rethink and perhaps change your choices. So many couples I have worked with have been so moved and excited by the wonderful collection of readings, they have a hard time picking their favorites! You may find that one part of a reading is exactly right for you, while the remainder of it is not. Simply cross out the lines you would like to omit. Feel free to adapt.

Throughout the following pages, in the margins here and there, you will also find brief quotes, snippets of written wisdom from a variety of sources. If you read one that speaks to you, by all means incorporate it into your ceremony. Or you might feature it on your birth announcement, your baby's blessing invitation, or your thank-you notes.

Consider this a guidebook. It will lead you step-by-step through the process of putting together a celebration that is just what you want. But you will find here something more as well. As an interfaith minister who has officiated at countless ceremonies, I have been blessed to be privy to these couples' deepest thoughts and feelings about becoming parents. With their approval, I include some of their informal remarks from their ceremonies— their feelings about their children, their thoughts about how they want to raise them, their dreams for their families. This is what brings it all home, up front and personal. This is what makes a personalized baby naming ceremony so special. Throughout the following pages, I have quoted the words of many of these happy parents, again with their approval, as they planned for and celebrated the welcoming of their child.

Let yourself be inspired. For there is an invisible parents' club to which you now belong, a common bond you share. That bond in a nutshell is this: our children come first. We love them more than life itself. We would give our lives for them if need be. This we would do without hesitancy, unconditionally. Is there any greater love?

PART I

First Steps

Chapter 1

WITH EACH CHILD, THE WORLD BEGINS ANEW!

A child enters into our midst, and face to face, hand to hand with this perfect creation, we are compelled to whisper, "It's a miracle." In this child we see infinite potential and we place our greatest hopes.

A baby reminds us from where we came. A baby takes us back to who we really are, before we accumulated all the layers of life. A child points to our innocence, to purity, and to glee, for only a baby has the capacity to laugh like that, at the sheer joy of being alive. When we witness a child's indescribable belly laugh, we rediscover who we are. As Christianity teaches: "Verily I say unto you, unless you become as little children, you shall not enter into the kingdom of heaven ... for of such is the kingdom of God." Simply put, children are closer to heaven.

Babies even smell like heaven! What parent does not rush home, perhaps from a hard day at work, yearning for the sweet smell of her newborn? With our noses nuzzled into the top of our babies' heads or in the crooks of our toddlers' necks, we feel we are home, right where the heart is. Embracing a child brings us back to what is truly important in life, and our day falls again into perspective. We experience a sense of inner peace and belonging.

When a child is born, all else in our lives seems to pale in comparison. Often we wonder what we did before having children that was really important. Life seems permanently divided into two parts: prebaby and postbaby. As one parent wrote to me, "I wish I could tell you how she has changed our lives, but I honestly can't remember what life was like before her. It is like all the questions have been answered." Can there be anything more life transforming?

3

And so, my heartfelt congratulations on the birth of your new baby! You have embarked on an exciting journey, one that will take you to places that you cannot even imagine at this point. For such a momentous rite of passage, many families feel a need to welcome and bless their children with a ceremony. With our hearts filled with gratitude for the gift of this newly arrived soul, it is a time to celebrate. Among the first questions on the minds of new parents is this one: How do we introduce our baby to our world and our world to our baby? If you are reading this book, this is probably the question on your mind right now. A baby welcoming, after all, is truly one of the handful of great and grand memorable events that span a lifetime, the passages that mark major family transitions.

I have led hundreds of such baby blessings, and these are absolutely my favorite ceremonies to perform because to me they represent pure and boundless joy. The grace I meet upon these children's faces, the presence of their families in my life, are the great gifts of my work. This is a work that makes the heart sing! As an ordained interfaith minister, I serve families from an amazing variety of backgrounds. They are nondenominational, interfaith, intercultural, multicultural, interracial, interdenominational, same faith, and humanist. Among them are traditionalists and nontraditionalists, the religious and nonreligious, liberals and conservatives. I spend time getting to know each of my families. And I have learned a great deal about the needs and wishes of modern-day parents.

Some are seeking ideas on how to plan and carry out a welcoming ceremony for their child that is nonreligious but spiritual in nature. Some wonder if it's possible to incorporate individualized elements within the traditional services and practices of the church, the synagogue, or the mosque. Others are faced with the need to honor and acknowledge different faiths and family traditions.

Many new parents looking for just such advice and suggestions have found me through my website and my previous book, *Joining Hands and Hearts*, about designing interfaith wedding ceremonies. Here is a small sampling from the e-mails I have received:

"What my husband and I know for sure is that we want our child to be honored and welcomed into this world properly and that we would like a ceremony based on love and life and in celebration of both families and our new joy."

"When we were married, we had a wonderful, inclusive wedding ceremony attended by my parish priest and a rabbi. We were really pleased with the nature of our ceremony, but we have not been able to find local resources in terms of raising an interfaith child or even how to conduct a naming ceremony that might be inclusive like our wedding."

"I've been trying to think ahead about a ceremonial celebration of the birth of our first baby. We are no longer affiliated with any church, but we believe in the sacred event of life and want to honor that somehow, in a powerful, connecting way that brings our families and friends together to celebrate the life of our child."

"This is our first child and we wish to create a ceremony for him that welcomes him into this world and celebrates his uniqueness. We particularly liked the idea you mention of a ceremony that honors family members and friends. You also state that your ceremonies have a universal context. This is especially important to us."

Do you hear echoes of your own hopes and concerns in those words?

Bless This Child is for you if you and your spouse are in a same-faith marriage, or if you are in an interfaith marriage, or if you and your partner are parents with no faith-based inclinations whatsoever. Our emphasis is on fashioning a personal, meaningful occasion that feels uniquely right to the people involved and that completely reflects your beliefs and wishes.

I call this a spiritual ceremony. Love is the key. We begin by focusing on the heart, on love, on that which is common to you and me and all life. Then we bring it up a notch—or two or three—to that which points to something greater than ourselves yet is in ourselves, to something sacred. Certainly, the birth of a child, and the ceremony that celebrates it, touches the sacred. After all, we are dealing with the miracle of life. Family is honored and embraced. Traditional aspects of baptisms and baby namings are celebrated in a universal context. All language is warm and inclusive. There is no judgment, agenda, or bias, no religious dogma.

In designing a child's welcoming ceremony, there can be no cookie-cutter solutions, for your family's tapestry is uniquely woven from many individual threads of personal, spiritual, religious, and cultural experiences and beliefs, past and present. Yet sadly, so many of life's rites of passage are punctuated by rote rituals. When I became an interfaith minister, I was determined that each ceremony I conducted would be deeply reflective

With each child, the world begins anew.

Midrash

of the spiritual and emotional enormity of what was going on with these particular participants. I believe it is my function as a celebrant to help bring all those gathered for the occasion from the everyday eating, drinking, walking life, into a sense of the sacred, and often into the transcendent. To do this, we must see with the eye of the heart, and I work hard to create ceremonies that pierce the heart.

With the information you find in these pages—readings, blessings, prayers, rituals, and the real-life stories of couples and their baby namings—

you can design and orchestrate your own ceremony, one to pierce the heart, one that completely reflects your family, beliefs, and cultural heritage.

It is my hope, too, that clergy from all faiths will use the material in this book, perhaps adapted to their own religion and particular needs, in their services.

If You Are an Interfaith Couple

It may interest you to know that approximately 30 million couples in the United States now live in interfaith households. Since there is little information available regarding baby ceremonies for these families, I have devoted a good portion of this book to the needs of the interfaith couple. You may have questions that so many of these parents ask me. What is an interfaith ceremony? What rituals can take place? Is it possible to have a baby blessing that will honor both traditions without offending our parents? Who will officiate? Where will it take place? Will our children be confused being raised in a two-faith household? Are there spiritual communities that welcome interfaith families? What support resources are available?

Over the following pages, we offer possible answers and solutions to these questions. The options are many, perhaps more than you know. I have no agenda. Nor do I take sides. My job is to serve your needs with the utmost love and care I can muster. When you are informed, you are better able to make choices that work best for your family. The answers lie with you, within the deep recesses of your soul.

Here is how I explained the concept of interfaith and the interfaith ceremony in my previous book, *Joining Hands and Hearts*:

> *Interfaith is not a religion. It walks among the religions. Interfaith begins when we create a bridge between one set of beliefs and traditions and another. We start by listening to each other and to the humanity in all of us. Interfaith emphasizes the universal principles and spiritual compassion taught by all schools of divinity and ethics. Each religion is an instrument for the divine, and together the world's religions form a glorious symphony. Interfaith is the acceptance and celebration of humankind in all its magnificent faiths, colors, cultures, and traditions. It is the acknowledgment that there is but one light that burns brightly through each faith and within each heart. In its essence, this light is love.*
>
> *In an interfaith ceremony we remember that it is love that transcends all. The spiritual teaching at the core of all religious traditions and humanist philosophies are emphasized. As Albert Einstein put it, "Remember your humanity!"*

Someone once asked me, "What are the beliefs of an interfaith minister?" I told him that I could only answer for myself, and this was my answer:

I believe that God, by whatever name, is that which exists within, connects, and binds us all. The late Unitarian minister and theologian Forrest Church expressed it in these words: "God is not God's name. God is our name for that which is greater than all and yet present in each." Yahweh, Christ, Allah, Brahman, Great Spirit, Chi, Love, Universal Spirit, Divine Presence—all are among the different names for God.

I believe that God has billions of faces and is always in front of you, everywhere.

I believe that the most important goal of every religion is to respect and revere all life, and in doing so, we revere God.

I believe that I do my job best when I help others find the transcendent in ordinary life, and in doing so, we hear the song of the universe.

Bottom line: the ceremonies within this book are rooted in love, the same love that brought your baby into this world in the first place.

I have had the privilege of working with people of all faiths, cultures, and colors. As I walk alongside these families through life's major rites of passage, I am aware that it is a sacred walking. This walking fills me with gratitude.

Take my hand, and we shall begin.

Chapter 2

THINKING ABOUT YOUR CEREMONY:
A QUESTIONNAIRE FOR PARENTS

When a couple first comes to me to begin talking about a naming ceremony for their child, they often are not quite certain just what they are seeking or what would be appropriate to their needs, their religious inclinations, and the wishes of older family members. Before we begin to sketch out some possibilities, I give them a questionnaire I have designed and suggest they review it.

Here, for you, is that questionnaire.

Read it over. Write in your responses. Fill it out with your partner, or have him or her complete his or her answers on a separate form. Here is a physical place for you to organize your wishes, feelings, and ideas, to put down on paper the guidelines that will help to shape the ceremony that evolves.

> Rejoice the singing of
> this new creation
> this wondrous thing
> this sacred gift
>
> *Kelly D. Matthews*

Take your time. Some of the questions will resonate with you; for others, you may not have anything specific to contribute. This is not a test. Not every space must be filled in. But I hope you do elect to complete as much of the questionnaire as possible, because I think you will find, as so many of my couples have reported, that this is a thought-provoking process and an enjoyable one, too. It will help you better articulate your needs—what you want and do not want in your baby's ceremony. Among other benefits, the questionnaire will encourage you to begin to consider how you wish to mention or involve family members.

What you will be doing is sketching out a rough framework into which can be fitted particular ceremonial elements, such as readings and prayers. In the course of thinking through and organizing your preferences, you are also creating a roadmap for the officiant who will eventually lead your ceremony. When it's completed, make a copy of it and bring it along when you meet with your officiant.

You will see that the questionnaire includes spaces for some nuts and bolts data: names, dates, time, place. These are concrete bits of information that obviously your officiant will need. But in addition, you will have the opportunity to express your innermost feelings about your child and how you see your roles as parents. If you wish, you may ask your celebrant (priest, minister, rabbi, imam, monk, or pundit) to include some of your responses as informal remarks at points in the ceremony. Or you yourself can read certain portions to your guests.

My heart melts when I read how much the parents I work with love their littlest angels! Indeed, many tell me that in greeting their child, they have met the meaning of their own existence. Children expand our capacity to love and help us grow exponentially. Indeed, the littlest ones among us become our greatest teachers. I always lace parents' responses from the questionnaire into the ceremonies I conduct, and the loving tenderness this creates in the room is palpable.

In the sample ceremonies in Part III of this book, I have included examples of how I incorporated parent questionnaire responses, for your reference and enjoyment. You and your celebrant can do the same, *if* that is what you wish. In hearing other families' testimonials about their newborn babies and young children, you may find your own feelings reflected in their words. They may touch home and inspire you.

While answering the questionnaire, and while reading my sample ceremonies later, you will realize, I believe, that a baby naming ceremony provides much opportunity for individuality, more than you might now imagine—the opportunity, for example, to convey the funny,

> **Before I formed you in the womb I knew you, Before you were born I set you apart.**
>
> *Jeremiah 1:5*

touching, heart-rending anecdotes and tales that make you, your child, and your family one of a kind. That is what a baby naming ceremony from the heart is all about.

One more thing: With the completed questionnaire, you have created a very special document that will gain meaning over time. I have learned from my couples that it is usually stored away, maybe in the "baby box" containing the important memory items from those first days and weeks. Imagine your grown child at some point reading his parents' most cherished hopes and dreams for him as his life began to take shape. Imagine her reading these words when she herself becomes a parent. That is the power of the questionnaire and its ultimate purpose. It is an effort you make now with rippling rewards into the future.

So settle back with a pencil and pad (of course, write directly on these pages, if space allows for your answer—this is your book!), a cup of tea or a glass of wine, and consider these:

Questions for Baby Welcoming, Baby Blessing, Baby Naming, Baby Dedication, or Universal Baptism

- Write down your child's full name.

- List your child's parents' full names, and the names of grandparents, great-grandparents, godparents or spiritual mentors (if applicable), siblings, and any other close family members or friends to be honored or included in the ceremony.

- List the date, time, place, and address of the ceremony.

- List your telephone numbers and e-mail addresses.

- Do you wish to honor/include the child's grandparents? Write a little about the grandparents and their relationships to their grandchild.

- Do you wish to honor/include your child's siblings in the ceremony? Write a little about them and their relationship with this child.

- Will your child be given godparents or spiritual mentors? If so, write a little about them. Why did you choose these particular individuals? What personal qualities/character traits do you hope they will share with your child?

- Is there anyone else you wish to specifically honor and include?

- Tell me about your spiritual, cultural, and religious backgrounds. Please tell me a little about your religious, spiritual, and/or philosophical beliefs.

- Do you believe in God? How do you perceive/feel God in your daily life?

- Are there any sensitive issues regarding family or religion I need to know about?

- How do you plan to raise your child spiritually and/or religiously?

- Does your child's name have special significance? Is there a reason you chose it?

- Will you also be giving your child a spiritual name/a Hebrew name/an Arabic name? What is it? Is there special significance to the name? Please elaborate.

- What is the significance of this ceremony for you? What do you hope to accomplish?

- Tell me about your child. What does this child mean to you? How do you love him/her? (Don't hold back! Count the ways!)

- What has your child done for your lives as individuals and as a couple?

- What does it mean to you to be a parent?

- Tell me about your spouse/partner as a parent.

- What do you pray/wish/dream/want for your child?

- How do you see your role as parents? What do you feel are your moral/spiritual responsibilities?

- What do you hope to teach your child?

- What aspects of your upbringing do you wish to emulate? What aspects do you *not* wish to emulate?

- Are there any funny, poignant, or spiritual stories about the conception or pregnancy or birth that you'd like to share at the ceremony?

- Are there any revealing stories regarding your child? Can you describe your child's emerging personality and habits?

- What do you wish to convey to everyone at this ceremony? What do you want to avoid?

- Are there any specific traditions, rituals, readings, prayers, or other items you know you want to include?

- Is there anything else your officiant should know?

When I give this questionnaire to the new parents I will work with, I end it with these words, which I now offer to you:

May angels watch over your journey as a family.

It is a blessed and exciting adventure.

Chapter 3

LOGISTICS: THE WHO, WHAT, WHERE, AND WHEN OF YOUR BABY BLESSING CEREMONY

As you begin to map out your plans, you may have a number of concerns regarding the logistics typically involved. In this chapter, I answer the most common questions I hear from parents.

When is it appropriate to have the ceremony?

I have performed baby blessings for children as young as a few days old and for children as old as three. Most blessings take place during the first year of the child's life, usually within the first six months. But new parents are often so overwhelmed by the vigorous demands of a newborn that they simply need a few months to adjust. Sometimes couples wait so long that they decide to delay even further, until a child's birthday, to mark the occasion. Others plan their ceremonies with me long before the child is due, and we then set the date for when he or she will be one, two, or three months old.

My feeling is that you should plan to have the ceremony as soon as you think you can get it all together. And it is never too late to be blessed!

Who will perform our ceremony?

If you are affiliated with a religious organization or if you have a special relationship with a clergy person, you can bring the ideas in this book to him or her. If you are not affiliated with an organization and you are in need of a celebrant, please see my resource directory at the end of this book, which will help you find an appropriate celebrant according to your wishes.

If you want a spiritual but nondenominational service, you might consider an interfaith minister or a Unitarian Universalist minister. Interfaith ministers will also co-officiate with other clergy. Many couples who have a traditional naming or baptism performed in their church, temple, or mosque have then asked me to lead a more personalized ceremony in their home. These babies were twice blessed.

Since baby blessings have no legal requirements, you have much leeway in creating your event. My advice: Carefully consider your options. Interview celebrants and follow your heart. You want to be certain that you make the right choice for your family. You want to be sure that you trust your celebrant to serve your needs.

> **Every child comes with the message that God is not yet discouraged with man.**
>
> *Rabindranath Tagore*

Besides the parents, child, and officiant, who should participate?

In most of the services I conduct, the child, parents, grandparents, godparents or spiritual mentors (if appointed), and the child's siblings all take part. All are included and honored. In some ceremonies, we have asked all the children at the gathering to come forward for a blessing, and this makes for a delightful moment. Just imagine it, in your mind's eye: all the little ones coming up to be blessed themselves or to offer a good wish for the new baby.

Sometimes, a special friend of the parents is recognized. In one case, a young mother wanted to honor her caregiver who stood by her side through her difficult infertility period, the pregnancy, the actual birth, and the early days that followed. We presented the caregiver with a gift along with a few personal words of thanks. Our honorary guest was moved to tears.

These are among the personal choices that create a customized event. Ultimately, you are the one who decides who will participate and/or be honored, and of course, there is absolutely nothing wrong with limiting the participants to parents, child, and officiant. The passages and rituals in Part II, the menu of elements, will help you make those decisions.

What will the ceremony look like?

A baby blessing can range from the traditional to the alternative. It can be religious, spiritual, humanist, cultural, or a mix. Based on your selection of rituals, prayers, blessings, and readings from our menu, your ceremony may evolve into a delightfully rich combination of features. If you want a nondenominational service that is not necessarily rooted in any tradition, you will find an abundance of passages and ceremonial elements to choose from. Most of my couples combine personal nondenominational elements with traditional ones that honor their respective backgrounds. In the words of Marianne Williamson, the popular author and lecturer on spirituality: "Let us create anew the rituals of ancient significance, with respect for ideas that have borne the tests of time and openness to new ideas that reflect the needs of our own era."

My suggestion: Simply circle the passages in the manual that appeal to you. After you have made your selections and have read the sample ceremonies in Part III, you will have a pretty clear idea of what your event will look like. Most of the couples I have worked with, as I mentioned earlier, do answer the questionnaire and ask me to include some of their personal words. In the sample ceremonies, you will see very specifically how this can be done and the fruits that it yields. You will learn how to incorporate the traditional alongside the more creative and individualized.

A personal customized ceremony touches the heart and draws the entire family into a warm embrace.

What should the event be called?

This is a question I am asked frequently, especially by interfaith couples.

Depending on the traditional elements you use, the ceremony typically is called a baby naming, a baptism, a christening, or a dedication, or some combination thereof.

A *baby naming* includes the tradition of formally naming the child. Sometimes the child is given an additional spiritual name, as is done in several faiths and cultures around the world; for example, in Judaism a Hebrew name is given.

A *baptism* involves a ritual of gently pouring water over the baby's head, as in the Christian tradition. In the Eastern Orthodox traditions, the child's body is immersed. I have conducted several ceremonies in which the child was completely immersed, and these were in the summer in a nearby stream, the warm ocean, or a small wading pool. Baptisms can be orchestrated in a universal sense. In a *universal baptism*, the baby is baptized simply as a child of God and welcomed as a child of humanity. This is essentially an initiation into this world. A *traditional baptism* is conducted in the name of the Father, Son, and Holy Spirit.

A *christening* is done in the name of Christ.

A baby *dedication* is a formal dedication of the child to God.

Some interfaith couples in which one is Christian shy away from a baptism altogether; others choose a universal baptism; still others elect to have a Christian baptism alongside a Jewish naming.

Many parents I have worked with simply refer to the event as a *baby blessing*. Still others have called it a *baby welcoming ceremony*. And one set of parents sent out invitations worded simply: "Please join us for a celebration of life, love, and friendship, honoring [their child's name]."

But you should be aware that the name might cause confusion among family members. In one family, the grandparents were devout Catholics; though perfectly accepting of their daughter's and son-in-law's decision to raise the grandchild interfaith, the grandmother talked about the baby's "baptism or whatever you call it," and wondered if a baby blessing "counts" as a baptism. In such a situation, some careful explanation ahead of time of what the ceremony will entail might be helpful.

Where should the ceremony take place?

I have led baby blessings in chapels, churches, synagogues, people's homes, and backyards; on decks, porches, rooftops, and balconies; in various rented banquet halls; and in nature's magnificence—in fields, woods, on mountain tops, and beside streams and the ocean. In short, a baby blessing can be held anywhere that feels right for you, your family, and your celebrant. After all, it is the sacred intention of the congregants that makes for a hallowed service. It is love that brings in the spirit of God.

If you are not affiliated with a religious organization, but you do, however, wish to have your ceremony in a church, chapel, or other religiously oriented site, you might consider renting a place of worship for the occasion. You can inquire into the chapels, churches, or temples nearest you. A fee or donation is required for the use of their premises for an allocated length of time. University chapels are often nondenominational and available to the public.

One more note: Quite often, arranging a ceremony for their child is the impetus for new parents to begin considering or seeking out a spiritual or religious community for their family, to carry them into the future. If you are thinking along those lines, this is a good time to do some research. Attend a service or two, meet the spiritual directors, pick up some literature, speak to the congregants, observe the children's religious education classes. When will you know you have found the spiritual or religious community for your family? You will feel it. It will feel like home.

What will we need for the ceremony?

There are some basics and some possible additional elements depending on the rituals you choose.

I usually ask for a *ceremonial table* that serves as an altar to hold candles, water, oil, kiddush cup or wine goblet, a basket filled with rose petals, the book I read from, and so on. A simple table covered with a white cloth is perfectly fine. Often, families make these areas quite lovely, sprinkling them with petals, draping fabric on the table, or decorating the table with bouquets of flowers. At one service, the parents placed an illustration of the family tree upon the table; at another, the child's parents put their own framed baby photos taken some thirty years earlier. After all, the ceremonial table or altar not only serves as a focal point during the ceremony, but helps to create a personal space. Sometimes nature provides a special altar—a large jutting rock by the ocean's shore or a beautiful slate boulder in the middle of the woods.

If you are planning a very extensive guest list, with the ceremony to be held in a large space, you should probably be sure that your celebrant will have access to a *microphone*.

Some rituals you may decide to include might require an additional display area and some "props." For example, grandparents or great-grandparents may give a gift item of personal significance at the ceremony—an old baby cup or the baseball Grandfather caught at Yankee Stadium, signed by all the players. Very often grandparents put together a scrapbook or shadow box featuring photos of family gatherings, Grandmother's famous kugel recipe, Grandfather's old war medals, Great-Grandpa's immigration papers, old and historic baby and wedding photos. This is the child's history. This is a grandparent's gift, and it can be displayed on a special table. Another favorite ritual that many parents choose: All present, including the youngsters, fill a basket with written and drawn best wishes for the baby being named that day. Crayons, colored markers, and papers are supplied.

Chairs can be provided for the parents—and godparents, if appointed—so that they may sit facing the congregation. I have led ceremonies in which all those attending have remained standing and in which all have been formally seated, as in a wedding. Sometimes only immediate family attends and sometimes there may be one hundred or more guests. Give some consideration to the length of the ceremony and to the comfort of the elderly. The oldest citizens among us often need to have a place to sit. In any case, they deserve to be seated! If the ceremony will be taking place at the height of summer, it might be thoughtful to have water bottles, fans, or parasols on hand. Or rent a tent.

My feeling is that everyone should be comfortable—including baby. I tell my parents: bring all that your baby loves—pacifier, bottle, toy, teething ring, bouncy chair, whatever. We want your child to be happy. It is okay for the front of the altar area to look like a baby's playroom! Playrooms are God's rooms. Baby's clothing, naturally, can be whatever is comfortable, though interestingly, many parents who have arranged even a nontraditional ceremony have dressed their baby in Mom's or Dad's or a grandparent's old christening gown. At one ceremony, the baby was clothed in a gown that had been passed down for eight generations in the family.

Do consider *music*. Music lifts the spirit and sets the tone for the occasion. It also helps create a sacred space. Including music can be as simple as appointing someone to play your favorite CD on a portable stereo. Of course, if you have a friend who plays an instrument, that's a lovely contribution to the moment. If you are in a church or synagogue, you can usually arrange for a brief performance by the house organist.

Sometimes a musical family member or friend will grace us with a song during the service. I have heard the voices of angels through solo performances dedicated to our babies of honor—and often the babies themselves seem transfixed by the beautiful sounds.

Music can open and end the ceremony. Solo, group performance, or quiet music may also punctuate and enhance the service at particular times, such as during a candle lighting. However you use it, choose music that touches the soul or that has meaning for you. I have watched guests smile and get teary-eyed as John Lennon's "Beautiful Boy" plays in the background as the parents and baby assemble. To conclude the ceremony, a celebratory sound is delightful. A number of my new parents have played Louis Armstrong's recording of "What a Wonderful World," which includes the charming words about watching babies grow.

In several ceremonies I've led, tech-savvy parents have set up a computer generated *slide show* depicting images of themselves and their child, perhaps shortly after the baby's birth or with other family members. This display is always a great hit with guests who enjoy commenting on the pictures while waiting for the ceremony to get underway.

If you need or desire a *baby blessing certificate*, perhaps a baptismal or naming certificate, check our directory at the end of this book where I have listed resources that supply these documents. Certificates are available for interfaith families as well. Visually, they vary in style from the official and simple to the sumptuous and creative. Carefully read the wording on the various forms offered and decide what is right for you and your celebrant. This document can be displayed, if you wish, on a small side table where the main players in the day's grand event will sign their names.

A *video* of the ceremony is almost *de rigueur* these days. Indeed, I recommend video recording to all my parents and to you. You do not need a professional videographer for this; a friend or family member can do the job.

In many ways, we strive to create a ceremony that will inspire the child throughout his lifetime, and the video is certainly a powerful factor. Imagine your child watching his grandparents blessing him and stating all they hope for him, on a day when those grandparents are no longer physically with him. Imagine your daughter someday watching her young parents talking of their love, hopes, and dreams for her. How special it will be for your child to see that you went to such loving effort to create an extraordinary and unique occasion to welcome her into the world. The video becomes something of a family heirloom that gets passed down the generations.

As this review of "logistics" suggests, many choices are available to you in designing not only the content—the words and rituals—but the who, what, where, and when elements of the ceremony.

Chapter 4

SENSITIVITIES AND CONSIDERATIONS
FOR THE INTERFAITH FAMILY

"I am looking to make a ceremony that will make all my family members happy."

This was a message I received from a new mother. It's a message—a fervent wish—that I frequently hear from parents who consult me. For many of these couples, the difficult issues revolve around how to design an event that adheres to their personal beliefs, while not upsetting or offending older and perhaps more tradition-bound relatives.

It can be done. And done properly, with great sensitivity, these occasions are enlightening experiences that not only "make family members happy," but can help unify individuals from different traditions. The hallmark of such a service is balance among the rituals, prayers, and blessings of the two—or more—traditions involved. I like to think of it as a sacred dance, one that goes back and forth in mutual love and respect.

A newborn babe brings light to the cottage, warmth to the hearth, and joy to the soul, for wealth is family, and family is wealth.

a Celtic saying

In one ceremony I led, the parents came from different Christian denominations, planned to raise their child in the Unitarian Church, and wanted a spiritual but nonreligious service to welcome and bless him. One of the grandmothers, an extremely devout woman who was devoted to her church, was understandably upset. The parents were aware of her unhappiness as they began to work out the details of their service. Among other supportive elements we included, we went to great lengths to honor the grandparents, including the grandmother's husband who had passed away. It all touched home. You can imagine my joy when, at the end of the day, she thanked me for "the most meaningful ceremony in my life." She had never before witnessed such a personalized service.

If you desire a blessing ceremony for your child that celebrates or honors both your religions, you may be surprised to discover just how little information is available to you. One reason for this state of affairs is that most religious organizations tend to shy away from interfaith family matters. Often they maintain the position that a couple should choose one religion in which to bless their baby and then require that the child be raised exclusively in that particular religion. For some families, this option works beautifully, especially when one parent is observant and the other is not.

Sometimes it is possible, depending on the requirements of your religion and the willingness of individual clergy members, to have clergy from both traditions bless the child. However, if your clergy person will not perform at an interfaith service, then do consider an interfaith minister for the event. The resource directory at the end of this book can help point you in the right direction in locating this individual. An interfaith minister will co-officiate baby blessing ceremonies with clergy of other religions, and this is how I have often been called to service. A blessing in these situations usually contains elements honoring both "sides." At one service in which I co-officiated with a rabbi mohel, the parents jokingly referred to their son's ceremony as a "brisening."

Having worked with both traditionalists and nontraditionalists and with many families that aim for an occasion that falls somewhere in between, my approach varies depending on the particular family. When you read through some of the sample services in Part III, you may notice that one is more Christian in slant or more Jewish. These were choices made by the parents themselves, as you too will make your own choices. Just think of the interfaith service as a sacred dance.

Some interfaith couples elect to have two separate ceremonies. In this way, the child is blessed in both faiths.

So let us discuss here the issues you should take into consideration in order to help ensure a memorable occasion. Again: Respect is the foundation. Love is the bridge.

Clarifying Your Feelings

Perhaps you will find that choosing the parts you want to include in a welcoming ceremony for your baby is not all that difficult. You will design an uplifting occasion that lasts for half an hour or one hour, to be followed by a party or happy gathering of friends and family, and you anticipate a lovely day.

Do not be surprised, however, if the planning process stirs up troublesome feelings, even some that take you by surprise. Maybe you or your partner are actually rather undecided about how to raise your child. Maybe you're feeling a little guilty, afraid of displeasing your parents. Or perhaps there is some deeper discomfort about your decisions. Perhaps you sense you are not being true to yourself.

Ideally, couples discuss these matters prior to joining their lives in marriage. Often, however, a baby naming is the first time two people actually sit down and begin to think about the issues surrounding children and religion, spirituality, ceremonial events—the first time the future becomes real. Becoming parents, as I mentioned earlier, marks the great divide, the before and after, the prebaby and postbaby lives, and religious or cultural feelings can become magnified when the anticipated child is actually born. They may be multilayered or subconscious.

Here is an example: Jen and Mark had agreed that their children would not be raised in a particular religion, though they intended to encourage spiritual understanding and development in various ways. When their son Jack was born, however, it suddenly became important to Jen that her child be given a Hebrew name. Mark was unhappy with this idea and protested. In counseling, Jen realized that what she really wanted was for her son to be named after her late father, a tradition that is often recognized in Judaism. The father's name was Solomon. So baby Jack became Jack Solomon, and the equivalent name in Hebrew was mentioned at his ceremony. Husband Mark came to recognize this as personally, spiritually, and culturally significant, while not religiously or legally significant.

As you talk over such issues, it's important that each partner feel heard—not judged, or looked down upon, or belittled. Neither of your points of view is better than the other; neither one matters more. As the Baha'i put it, "The world of humanity is possessed of two wings, male and female. As long as these two wings are not equivalent in strength, the bird will not fly." As I often tell the couples I work with, "Watch your tone." Try to express even your strongest or most difficult feelings with compassion. Be kind always. Trust in the strength of your love.

Professional counseling, perhaps with a spiritual advisor, can help tremendously if you and your partner are coming to grips with differences between the two of you. If you are not united, you are potentially alienating your partner, and that can cause disharmony and stress in your marital relationship as well as in your extended family. In Part IV, "Down the Years:

Raising Your Child in Spiritual Wisdom," you will find some thoughts that may be helpful for you to consider at this juncture.

And most importantly as you plan for the big day, you need to be reconciled in your differences before approaching your parents.

Giving birth and nourishing, having without possessing, acting with no expectations, leading and not trying to control: this is the supreme virtue.

Tao Te Ching

Informing the Grandparents

This may be a particularly thorny issue in your family constellation. Understandably, many grandparents will be disappointed if you do not have a traditional ceremony that follows exclusively in their faith. They may be suspicious, disapproving, or resistant. Indeed, they may feel that their way of life, their beliefs and culture, is being lost, even annihilated. Often, grandparents blame a son-in-law/daughter-in-law for influencing their child. Some feel that their child should persuade his or her spouse toward their religion.

Beware of any divisive behavior from your parents! Such tactics should be dealt with immediately, lovingly, but firmly. That is why it is so important that you clarify feelings between the two of you and come to your own conclusions before approaching your parents.

If you are having an interfaith ceremony and are planning to raise your child in both traditions, it is best if you explain your decisions to your parents with courage and caring. Address their concerns honestly and openly.

One of my favorite mottoes is, "When in doubt, do the loving thing." And sometimes the loving thing is to set boundaries. Remember that fear does not a bridge make; only love can do that. Love takes courage. The word courage actually comes from the Latin root word *cor*, which means heart. *Cor* + age literally means "more at heart." Courage is facing your fears and trepidations—and your parents—with all your heart.

When you do talk to nana or yaya (yia-yia in the Greek), present a united front as a couple. Begin by saying, "We have decided ..." or "It is our wish ..." Avoid sending mixed signals. Explain how the ceremony will go. At the same time, understand that it can be difficult—in fact, sometimes *excruciating*—for the older generation to realize that a grandchild will be raised in another faith or in a combination of religious traditions; be sensitive to those feelings. I ask my couples to put themselves in their parents' position. Often the thoughts and beliefs of one generation do not extend into the next, and grandparents' discomfort with that fact needs to be respected.

I remember one evangelical Christian grandmother who announced that she would not attend her grandson's bris. She told her daughter and son-in-law that this decision in no way changed her love for them or her grandchild. She simply would not be comfortable going to the ceremony. The parents of the baby asked my advice. As they informed me that there had been clear and honest communication between mother and daughter, my advice was to respect the grandmother's feelings. She loved them but would not be present at the welcoming ceremony.

Occasionally, grandparents remain intractable. A Russian Orthodox/ Jewish couple called me for advice. Their daughter would be raised in the father's Jewish tradition, and they did not know how to respond to Galina's mother, who refused to attend the child's naming ceremony, which would be conducted by a rabbi, and now threatened to never visit them again. It was obvious from our conversation that the decision to bring up their child in the Jewish faith was as much Galina's as her husband's. She really no longer felt tied to the Russian Church and, in fact, leaned more toward Eastern philosophy. Since Galina had already spoken extensively to her mother, I suggested she write her a letter explaining her beliefs. Feelings and thoughts are often better articulated, structured, and presented in this way. In her letter, Galina would also express the hope that her mother would continue to be involved in the life of her grandchild.

In Part IV, we will explore further this matter of hurtful disapproval from the older generation, and what might be done about it. For now, just remember that how you will raise your children is, of course, up to you and your partner. I often quote Joseph Campbell, the late writer and lecturer in comparative religions, to young couples: "If you are married and your marriage doesn't come first, then you really aren't married." Your spouse and your children are your first priority. Some grandparents need to hear this in no uncertain terms.

At your ceremony itself, let there be no unpleasant surprises!

In the following several areas, what is done or said, or what is not done or not said, can make a big difference in carrying out a ceremony that makes everyone happy.

Working closely with your celebrant is critical in this regard, for that individual can be an informative and soothing bridge as he or she explains elements that may be unfamiliar to the older generation. I have walked into many situations that began in fear and distrust from both sides, only to end in tremendous relief and often joy. Why? Because we honored without offending. We remembered our humanity, and we put love first.

The Importance of Language and Symbols

Language must give discomfort to no one. In interfaith services in particular, we need to be highly sensitive to both sides of the families, especially observant grandparents and great-grandparents who might be offended by the use of certain words or rituals. In those services, for example, God is usually referred to universally as God. Those present can then affirm God in their hearts by whatever name they use.

On the other hand, I have officiated at ceremonies in which I have been asked to speak of Jesus's and Allah's teachings. I have led ceremonies in which the child was given a Hebrew name, the blessing over the wine was done in Hebrew, *and* we recited the Lord's Prayer and baptized the child in the name of the Father, Son, and Holy Spirit. These are the exceptions, however. Typically, God is invoked and praised simply as God. Or perhaps the ceremony you devise is humanist in nature, one that feels spiritual but omits the word God entirely.

When making your decision about where you will have your ceremony, again consider if the setting will feel comfortable to your guests. Most interfaith couples choose neutral ground—in homes, backyards, rented banquet halls, and so on, or in nondenominational chapels that are unadorned, without religious icons. There are, of course, always exceptions. I have led interfaith Jewish/Christian baby blessings in both churches and temples, including some that were filled with specific religious symbols. Those were decisions the couples themselves made.

When there is room in the heart, there is room in the house.

a Danish proverb

The Officiant's Presentation

What your officiant wears and how he or she will be addressed may be a sensitive issue. For example, my robes contain no religious symbols. I am also aware of the importance of color. I wear blue and white if working with a Jewish/Christian couple. I wear my red and gold prayer stole if one or both sides of the family is Chinese, Japanese, or Indian, as red is considered an auspicious color and signifies good luck. I wear only a simple white robe if working with a Muslim/Christian family.

If the couple I'm working with feels that my title—Reverend—might bother the grandparents, I suggest everyone refer to me simply by my first name and as "the officiant," on the invitations and in person on the day itself.

Choosing Godparents

Appointing godparents for a child is rooted in both Jewish and Christian traditions, though the meaning attached is somewhat different. It is customary to have two godparents, but I have led ceremonies in which there were as many as thirteen. Wonderful! In my opinion, we can never have too many spiritual mentors in life.

If you are Christian and religiously observant, you may want the godparents to be of your faith. For an interfaith couple—such parents often prefer the term spiritual mentors or life mentors—a considerate choice might be godparents from both sides of the family. Many pick godparents for their personal qualities of character and integrity.

Think carefully about your choices and about what matters most to you. One of my couples, Catholic/Episcopal parents who had their universal baby blessing conducted in a Unitarian Universalist chapel, had four Jewish godparents. These individuals were chosen for their spiritual strength and obviously not for their faith. Another interfaith couple chose two Christian godparents, two Jewish godparents, and a Native American godmother. At the service, a traditional gift of the Turtle Clan, a beaded leather pouch, was presented to the baby. Godmother had lovingly created the pouch herself, saying a prayer as she sewed on each bead. She then asked me to read a Native American prayer, after which we all shouted a one-word Native American chant, something equivalent to our "Amen" or "Hallelujah." Everyone was really quite moved, including me.

For interfaith parents, the baby welcoming ceremony may be the first of many decisions you'll be making as your child grows. In Part IV, "Down the Years: Raising Your Child in Spiritual Wisdom," we'll talk more about what works best both for children and for the blended families they grow up in.

PART II
The Baby Blessing Ceremony:
A Menu of Elements

READINGS, PRAYERS, BLESSINGS, RITUALS, AND QUOTES

A couple contacted me to help them design and then to officiate at a blessing for their new son. After looking through the selections I presented to them, this young mother sent me an e-mail message: "We feel a little overwhelmed by the choices—they were all so good! We picked things we liked, but we're not sure how they fit in."

In this section, I present you with the same menu of elements, a cornucopia of those "so good" choices. This is the most complete manual of readings, prayers, blessings, and rituals available for baby ceremonies, and full of traditional and creative ideas, options, and solutions. Here, and in Part III, you will see just how they can be arranged, with much room for adaptation and personalization.

In baby ceremonies, there are no hard-and-fast rules as to which elements go first, second, and third, with some exceptions—for example, the celebrant's welcoming words obviously open a ceremony and the baby's formal naming is usually done toward the beginning. After her welcoming words, your celebrant may recite a general blessing or invocation or an honored guest may recite a reading selected by the parents. I prefer to hold off a baptism until toward the end, as sometimes the baby will cry—though often, if the water is warm, the little angels actually enjoy it. In fact, older children often actively participate.

The structure you settle on depends somewhat on the features you choose. So read through the following pages with pencil in hand, and circle the passages and rituals that have meaning for you, that pierce your heart or make you smile. When you make your selections and have in mind a design that pleases you, you can bring those passages to the celebrant of your choice.

Be careful not to choose too much—a temptation for many couples. Consider the length of your ceremony. Do you want it to be twenty minutes, half an hour, one hour? The choice is yours, and here is a helpful rule of thumb: Four single-spaced typed pages typically translate to a twenty- to twenty-five-minute ceremony. Eight single-spaced typed pages translate to a forty- to fifty-minute ceremony. Another helpful rule of thumb: I usually suggest that my couples look for a maximum of two to three readings, two to three rituals, and two to three blessings. Of course, this varies.

I'm suggesting you use a pencil, because you can erase as you come nearer to completion and edit your choices. Feel free to change, delete, or adapt words to suit your needs.

Begin circling!

Processional

Often, though not always, the baby is formally carried in by the parents. Sometimes I lead the procession, followed by the parents with the baby and the baby's siblings if they are young (older siblings can walk behind their parents). Then enter the godparents or spiritual mentors, if appointed, and the grandparents, though often the grandparents or godparents are already seated and remain so. At other occasions, I have waited for the family at the altar or designated ceremonial table.

Do consider music at this stage. It sets the mood and helps to create a sacred space. Typically, classical music is played, but on occasion, the choice reflects the cultural or religious backgrounds of the participants. The music might be more contemporary or light-hearted. One set of modern-minded parents chose to process holding their daughter to Stevie Wonder's "Isn't She Lovely." If your baby has older siblings, they can walk ahead of you ringing handbells, which makes for a wonderful chiming spectacle.

Think about what would be most comfortable for you and what makes sense depending on the location of the ceremony.

Welcoming Words

Here are a few selections of my own opening words and some (as indicated) written by others. You will find adapted versions, laced with the couples' own words, in our sample ceremonies in Part III.

Selection 1

Einstein once said that we could live life in one of two ways: as if nothing is a miracle or as if everything is a miracle. Who can deny a newborn child as a living miracle? So, it is with overwhelming gratitude for the divine gift that is their child that [parents' names] have gathered you, their cherished family and friends, for this ceremony. Today, we will bless him, welcome him into our community, this mystical union of souls on earth. Together we will express our gratitude for the gift that he truly is. In him we see infinite potential and we place our greatest hopes.

Selection 2

Kahlil Gibran once wrote: "Keep me away from the wisdom which does not cry, the philosophy which does not laugh, and the greatness which does not bow before children." Today I ask us all to bow our heads before the power that is a child. Will you stand with us with a little bit of awe at the gift

35

that is a child? If anyone should doubt the power of a child, just watch what happens when a baby is brought into the room. Without a word, all attention goes toward the baby. So today, with great joy in our hearts, we have come to give thanks for [child's name]. Today, [parents' names] have gathered their beloved family and friends—all of you—to honor, welcome, and celebrate their daughter as the unique soul that she is. We are called here today to honor this child as a divine manifestation and a living representative of God upon this earth.

Selection 3

Thank you all for standing by this family's side for [child's name] blessing ceremony. [Parents' names] are so grateful for the great gift of their baby, as well as for the gift of family and friends. Every heart filled with love increases God's presence. So please go to your hearts for this ceremony and open them as wide as you can. Fill yourselves with the glory of God, the beauty that is within you and that which is all around you—everywhere! To quote a spiritual teacher: "The winds of grace are always blowing. But you have to raise the sails!"

Let's raise the sails as we come together now with a united purpose—a holy bond of intent—to give thanks for the gift that is [child's name]. Today, we will bless him, anoint him, and welcome him into our spiritual community, the spiritual community we call humanity, the mystical union of souls on earth. A new child has come into the world. We rejoice for him, his parents, his grandparents, and for all of us whose lives will assuredly be enriched by his arrival.

> **Every person born into the world represents something new, something that never existed before, something original and unique.**
>
> *Martin Buber*

Selection 4

Why is a young child so magical? Children are the closest things we have to heaven on earth. [Child's name] represents pure joy and pure potential. She brings us back to a time when there was only hope, trust, and innocence. A child returns us all, and particularly his or her parents, to the best of our own childhood. We all need to be more like [child's name] in her openness and happiness. We need to remember to laugh and play like children. That is the great gift children give to us. They bring us back to joy! Picasso once said that he spent years trying to relearn how to draw like a child. There is great wisdom and inspiration in children, if we only listen. Look into a baby's eyes and you will see something that perhaps you have forgotten. There is so much God in children.

Today we have come together to welcome young [child's full name] and to acknowledge the divinity that exists within her. Today we will give thanks for the gift of her presence amongst us. We will bless her and welcome her into our spiritual community. Today we will also pray for guidance for the watchkeepers of her soul—her parents—and indeed for all those who will touch her life—all of you—who will help nurture her in realizing beauty, majesty, and grace—God's potential within her, on this, the great path of the human being.

Selection 5

Carl Sandburg once wrote, "A child is God's opinion that the world should go on." Is there anything in life that gives us more hope than the birth of a child? Is there anything that motivates a parent more to live, to push on, than his or her child? [Child's name] was born to [parents' names] on [date of birth], and we rejoice. It is for these reasons that we feel a need to formally celebrate this new life in our midst with a ceremony. Today we will welcome his arrival into our community with heads bowed in gratitude. We bless [child's name], for in him we see infinite potential and we place our greatest hopes. He is our future.

Selection 6 *[from Rev. Michael Ingersoll]*

There is nothing as seemingly ordinary and yet as wonderfully extraordinary as the birth of a child. In her the world is reborn. Through her we see yesterday absolved, new horizons opened, and the certainty of change. We are stilled into silence as we witness the miracle of a new life unfold. This is the premise of all life—the beginning.

So we are gathered here today with this man and this woman in celebration of their child's entrance into the world. You all have been invited, because as family and closest friends, your involvement and continued interest will always be welcomed in this child's life.

Selection 7 *[adapted from Rev. Miranda Holden, Director, the Interfaith Seminary UK]*

The purpose of a baby blessing is to consciously sanctify the entrance of a soul into the world, that this soul might walk through life remembering his true essence. Today we give thanks for the miracle of new life, the life that is [child's name]. Today we also acknowledge the sacred role of [child's name]'s parents, grandparents, and godparents as guardians offering unconditional love, acceptance, and wisdom to this new generation. Finally, we acknowledge and honor the interconnectedness of this child with the larger community, and indeed with all of creation. With hearts filled with joy and gratitude, we formally celebrate [child's name]'s presence among us.

Selection 8 [opening words specifically for a Judeo-Christian ceremony]

This is a ceremony to formally mark the naming of this child. It is a time when we welcome this precious being, born of God and of earth, into our hearts, into this loving community of family and friends, and into the family of all creation.

Why celebrate and mark the giving of a name? What is a deeper meaning of this act?

In the book of Genesis, after God had created the world he invited Adam to name all the creatures and plants that had been created. In this act, the act of naming, Adam became a cocreator with God. And through the act of naming, Adam was given loving stewardship over what he had named. He became responsible for the care and well-being of all that he had named.

And so symbolically, in naming a child, parents accept this same sacred trust—to enter into partnership with God to care for and watch over the life, growth, and welfare of this precious and perfect expression of God's love made manifest to us.

Selection 9 [interfaith couples may wish to add these words to the selections above]

[Child's name] will grow up with the knowledge of two traditions, and for this he is twice blessed. [Mother's name] and [father's name] have each selected elements that honor their spiritual and personal beliefs and that reflect who they are as a family, and we have woven them into this baby blessing ceremony. It is our hope that [child's name], through his parents' example, will learn the meaning of respect, tolerance, and understanding. We pray that the world [child's name] inherits will be one of peace. And if not, we pray that he will be one of the peacemakers.

READINGS

After the welcoming words, there may be a reading or opening blessing, which can be delivered by your celebrant or by an honored guest. Having a family member or friend give a reading is a lovely way to include someone special in your ceremony.

Readings tell your family and friends how you feel about your child or spiritual beliefs. They should reflect you—what is in your heart. The selections on these pages are organized according to secular poetry and prose, scripture, and blessings/prayers. They represent some of humanity's literary gems. Enjoy!

Poetry and Prose

Selection 1 *[from* The Prophet, *"On Children," by Kahlil Gibran]*
And a woman who held a babe against her bosom said, Speak to us of
    Children.
And he said:
Your children are not your children.
They are sons and daughters of Life's longing
for itself.
They come through you but not from you,
And though they are with you yet they belong
not to you.
You may give them your love but not your
thoughts,
For they have their own thoughts.
You may house their bodies but not their souls,
For their souls dwell in the house of tomorrow,
which you cannot visit, not even in your
dreams.
You may strive to be like them,
but seek not to make them like you.
For life goes not backward nor tarries with
yesterday.
You are the bows from which your children as
living arrows are sent forth.
The archer sees the mark upon the path of the
infinite,
and He bends you with His might
that His arrows may go swift and far.
Let your bending in the archer's hand be for
gladness;
for even as He loves the arrow that flies,
so He loves also the bow that is stable.

Selection 2 *[by Bryce Courtenay; a good reading for grandparents]*
You were formed with perfect feet and hands
and a heart that beats nonstop,
sometimes for a hundred years.
You inherited a thousand generations
of wisdom, skill, poetry, song,
all the sunrises and sunsets of knowledge past.

You are the sum of all the people
who went before you.

Selection 3, *author unknown*
We believe in children—little ones, big ones,
thin ones, and chubby ones.
There is faith in their eyes, love in their touch,
hope in their attitude.
We thrill with them at life's little joys,
bow to them in worship
and hold them close in tragedy.
We believe in children, the fragile dream of yesterday,
life's radiant reality today
and vibrant substance of tomorrow.
We believe in children, for wherever we go,
we find yesterday's children who were nurtured in love,
truth and beauty at work trying to make this world
a better place for everyone.

Selection 4 *[from Francis Thompson and William Blake; a good reading before or after a baptism]*
Know you what it is to be a child? It is to have a spirit yet streaming from the waters of baptism; it is to believe in love, to believe in loveliness, to believe in belief; it is to be so little that the elves can reach to whisper in your ear; it is to turn pumpkins into coaches, and mice into horses, lowness into loftiness, and nothing into everything—for each child has a fairy godmother in his or her own soul; it is to live in a nutshell and count yourself the king or queen of infinite space; it is:
To see the World in a grain of sand,
And a heaven in a wildflower,
Hold infinity in the palm of your hand,
And eternity in an hour.

Selection 5 *[by Rabbi Rami M. Shapiro; a good reading for parents]*
We are humbled by the awesome responsibility of this moment.
We are filled with joy and trembling
as we contemplate the tasks that lie before us:
Modeling love, teaching courage,
Instilling honesty, integrity and responsibility.
May we come to embody the virtues we teach,

and may our child see in us,
The values and behaviors we hope to see in him.

Selection 6, *author unknown*

Give us the spirit of the child.
Give us the child who lives within—the child who trusts, the child who
imagines, the child who sings, the child who receives without reservation,
the child who gives without judgment.
Give us a child's eyes, that we may receive the beauty and freshness of this
day like a sunrise.
Give us a child's ears, that we may hear the music of mythical times.
Give us a child's heart, that we may be filled with wonder and delight.
Give us a child's faith, that we may be cured of our cynicism.
Give us the spirit of the child, who is not afraid to need, who is not afraid to
love.

Selection 7 *["My Wish for You" by Kathleen Haeny]*

In my wish, you would be blessed
with friendships, happy and long.
Foundations would form in your life
to make you kind, caring and strong.
Curiosity would fill contented days,
creating respect, integrity and cheer.
The sun would rise with fresh adventures,
celebrating new chapters of your years.
In my wish, you would feel passion
for goodness, knowledge and trust.
Your life would be the model of one
that's upright, giving and just.
Into your heart, belief would be planted
that won't falter, fade or grow old.
You would reflect charity and trust
and blossom with the spirit in your soul.

Selection 9 *[by James McBride]*

Love is the most democratic act imaginable. It is the great equalizer. Not
everyone has the opportunity, luck, or skill to become a great filmmaker,
architect, businessman, artist, or professor. But everyone with the courage to
love can earn the privilege of sitting on a park bench and having someone—a
child, a granddaughter, an adopted son—stroke their hand and say, "You're

the greatest thing that has ever happened to me." That is the ultimate test of greatness, the ultimate test of freedom, the ultimate rebellious act. That kind of love, family love, makes us powerful beyond measure.

Selection 11 *[by Marianne Williamson]*

Our deepest fear is not that we are inadequate. Our deepest fear is that we are powerful beyond measure. It is our light, not our darkness that most frightens us. We ask ourselves, who am I to be brilliant, gorgeous, talented, and fabulous? Actually, who are you not to be? You are a child of God. Your playing small doesn't serve the world. There is nothing enlightened about shrinking so that other people won't feel insecure around you. We are born to make manifest the glory of God that is within us. It is not just in some of us, it's in everyone. And when we let our own light shine, we unconsciously give other people permission to do the same. As we are liberated from our own fear, our presence automatically liberates others.

Selection 12 *[by Mozelle Schouten LeBlanc]*

If the Father in Heaven should say unto me,
"I will grant thee one wish, Mozelle.
So thou hadst best think deeply and long
so thou wilt wish wisely and well."
I'd not ask the Lord for a wonderful voice
or for great fame untold.
I'd not ask for a beautiful face
Or for the glitter of gold.
I'd ask for something far greater than these,
The greatest gift from above.
Just a wee thing I could call all my own,
A dear little baby to love.
A dear little hand clasped tight in my own,
A dear mouth made for me to kiss.
Of all the great things that the Lord could bestow
What gift could be greater than this?

Selection 13 *["Children Learn What They Live" by Dorothy Law Nolte; some of us have grown up with these words tacked up on the refrigerator door!]*

If children live with criticism,
They learn to condemn.
If children live with hostility,
They learn to fight.

If children live with ridicule,
They learn to be shy.
If children live with shame,
They learn to feel guilty.
If children live with encouragement,
They learn confidence.
If children live with tolerance,
They learn to be patient.
If children live with praise,
They learn to appreciate.
If children live with acceptance,
They learn to love.
If children live with approval,
They learn to like themselves.
If children live with honesty,
They learn truthfulness.
If children live with security,
They learn to have faith in themselves and others.
If children live with friendliness,
They learn the world is a nice place in which to live.

Section 14, *author unknown*
Our family is a circle of strength and love.
With every birth and every union the circle grows.
Every joy shared adds more love,
Every crisis faced together
Makes the circle grow stronger.

Section 15 *[by Sophia Lyon Fahs]*
And so the children come.
And so they have been coming.
Always in the same way they come,
Born of the seed of man and woman.
No angels herald their beginning,
No prophets predict their future courses,
No wise men see a star to point their way
To find the babe that may save [hu]mankind.
Yet each night a child is born is a holy night.
Fathers and Mothers—
Sitting beside their children's cribs—

Feel glory in the wondrous sight of a life beginning.
They ask: "When or how will this new life end?
Or will it ever end?"
Each night a child is born is a holy night.

Selection 15 *[an Omaha Native American reading]*
Sun, Moon, Stars, all you that move in the heavens, hear us!
Into your midst has come a new life.
Make his/her path smooth, that he/she may reach the brow of the first hill!
Winds, Clouds, Rain, Mist, all you that move in the air, hear us!
Into your midst has come a new life.
Make his/her path smooth, that he/she may reach the brow of the second hill!
Hills, Valleys, Rivers, Lakes, Trees, Grasses, all you of the earth, hear us!
Into your midst has come a new life.
Make his/her path smooth, that he/she may reach the brow of the third hill!
Birds, great and small, that fly in the air,
Animals, great and small, that dwell in the forest,
Insects that creep among the grasses and burrow in the ground, hear us!
Into your midst has come a new life.
Make his/her path smooth, that he/she may reach the brow of the fourth hill!
All you of the heavens, all you of the air, all you of the earth, hear us!
Into your midst has come a new life.
Make his/her path smooth, then shall he/she travel beyond the four hills!

Selection 16 *[*The Parent's Tao Te Ching *by William Martin]*
You do not know the true origin of your children.
You call them yours
but they belong to a greater Mystery.
You do not know the name of the Mystery,
but it is the true Mother and Father of your children.
At birth your children are filled with possibilities.
It is not your job to limit these possibilities.
Do not say, "This is possible for you.
These other things are not."
They will discover on their own what is and is not possible.
It is your job to help them stay open
to the marvelous mysteries of life.

Selection 18

The Kabbalah, the Jewish book of mysticism, states that before a child is born, an angel presses her smallest finger to the baby's lip and whispers, "Shhhh. Tell no one!" The indentation of the angel's finger remains on the child's upper lip. If we look in the mirror and at one another, we can still see this reminder upon our lips. It reminds us from where we all come.

Selection 19 *[by Ysaye Maria Barnwell]*

For each child that's born
a morning star rises and sings to the universe
who we are
We are our grandfather's prayers
We are our grandmother's dreamings
We are the breath of the ancestors
We are the spirit of God
We are
Mothers of courage
Fathers of time
Daughters of dust
The sons of great visions
Brothers of love
Lovers of life
Builders of nations
Keepers of faith
Makers of peace
Wisdom of ages ...

Selection 20 *[Readings 20, "If," by Rudyard Kipling, and 21 are often read at Coming of Age ceremonies. However, a parent, godparent, or grandparent has on occasion read them at baby blessings.]*

If you can keep your head when all about you
Are losing theirs and blaming it on you,
If you can trust yourself when all men doubt you
But make allowance for their doubting too,
If you can wait and not be tired by waiting,
Or being lied about, don't deal in lies,
Or being hated, don't give way to hating,
And yet don't look too good, nor talk too wise:
If you can dream—and not make dreams your master;
If you can think—and not make thoughts your aim;

If you can meet with triumph and disaster
And treat those two imposters just the same;
If you can bear to hear the truth you've spoken
Twisted by knaves to make a trap for fools,
Or watch the things you gave your life to broken,
And stoop and build 'em up with wornout tools;
If you can make one heap of all your winnings
And risk it on one turn of pitch-and-toss,
And lose, and start again at your beginnings
And never breathe a word about your loss;
If you can force your heart and nerve and sinew
To serve your turn long after they are gone,
And so hold on when there is nothing in you
Except the will which says to them: "Hold on";
If you can talk with crowds and keep your virtue,
Or walk with kings—nor lose the common touch,
If neither foes nor living friends can hurt you;
If all men count with you, but none too much,
If you can fill the unforgiving minute
With sixty seconds worth of distance run,
Yours is the Earth and everything that's in it,
And—which is more—you'll be a Man, my son.

Selection 21, *author unknown*
A strong woman works out every day to keep her body in shape …
but a woman of strength kneels in prayer to keep her soul in shape.
A strong woman isn't afraid of anything …
but a woman of strength shows courage in the midst of her fear.
A strong woman won't let anyone get the best of her …
but a woman of strength gives the best of herself to everyone.
A strong woman makes mistakes and avoids the same in the future …
but a woman of strength realizes life's mistakes can also be God's blessings
    and capitalizes on them …
A strong woman walks surefootedly …
but a woman of strength knows God will catch her when she falls.
A strong woman wears the look of confidence on her face …
but a woman of strength wears grace.
A strong woman has faith that she is strong enough for the journey …
but a woman of strength has faith that it is in the journey that she will
    become strong.

Selection 22 *[by Mary Knight, author of* Love Letters Before Birth and Beyond*]*

This birth, this new life is not our first meeting, nor is this our first home. The welcome our hearts sing to you, oh round-faced one, has echoed down a thousand years. Here we are again, old friend, falling in love with you. Teach us your ways so that we may create ourselves anew. Teach us how to wonder and play, to greet the day with eyes so wide open that the world falls in. Teach us how to let go of everything that isn't love, oh infinite soul of our soul, one more time, so that we may know who we are.

Selection 23 *[from Momma Zen, by Karen Miller]*

Of course you love your spouse. You love your parents and brothers and sisters. You love your friends. You love your home and perhaps your hometown. You love your dog. You may love your work. You might attest to loving your alma mater, mashed potatoes, or reading on a rainy day.

But this is love. The feeling you have for a child is so indescribably deep and consuming that it must qualify as one of the few transcendent experiences in your plain old ordinary life. It is miraculous and supreme and irrevocable. It makes all things possible.

First, life is not what you think it is. What you call life is not yours at all—not yours to plan, manipulate, or control, at least not very often. That's a staggering realization. If life wasn't mine, what was it? In fleeting moments of deep satisfaction and insight, I saw the absolute truth of life: the unbroken line of love that led to my existence and would lead on through my daughter. My mother and father's love, her mother and father's love, and back and back forever ago. Love that is no mere word, love that goes beyond feeling, love that is life itself. I was filled with a rush of respect for all parents everywhere. This was how we all got here. What miracles, what sacrifice, what love! I never knew, nor could I have, before now. Can you imagine this love? Can you anticipate it, fabricate it, measure and evaluate it? No you can't; you can only be love, and your child will release its magnitude within you.

Turns out you can take or leave mashed potatoes. No matter how miserable I was at the moment, I knew that life itself was overwhelmingly and infinitely good. This is the balm for all the bad days ahead. This is the only fix. This is the source and strength that lifts you bottom out time and again.

Just love.

Selection 24 *[from the* Tao Te Ching *by Lao Tzu]*
Giving birth and nourishing,
having without possessing,
acting with no expectations,
leading and not trying to control:
this is the supreme virtue.

Selection 25 *["A Wish for You, Our Child," by Donna Dargis]*
If there could be only one thing
in life for us to teach you,
we would teach you to love.
To respect others
so that you may find respect in yourself.
To learn the value of giving,
so that if ever there comes a time
in your life that someone really needs,
you will give.
To act in a manner that you would wish to be treated.
To be proud of yourself.
To laugh and smile as much as you can,
in order to help bring joy
back into this world
To have faith in others.
To be understanding.
To stand tall in the world and
to learn to depend on yourself.
To take from this Earth
those things which you really need,
so there will be enough for others.
To not depend on money or material things
for your happiness, but
to learn to appreciate the people
who love you, the simple beauty
that God gave you, and to find peace
and security within yourself.
To you, our child, we hope we will teach all these things,
For they are love.

Selection 26 *[by Rainer Maria Rilke; a good reading for a godparent]*
Have patience with everything unresolved in your heart
and try to love the questions themselves ...
Don't search for the answers,
Which could not be given to you now,
Because you would not be able to live them.
And the point is, to live everything.
Live the questions now.
Perhaps then, someday far in the future,
Live your way into the answer.

Selection 27 *[by Gary Zukav, adapted]*
The soul is the mother ship and you are part of the fleet. When you don't sail in the direction of your soul, you are lost and you have the feeling, "Is that all there is?" But when you sail in the direction that your soul is leading you, you become aligned with your soul, you gain momentum, you feel meaning in your life. Meaning is our inner compass.

Scripture

Psalm 36: 8-10 *[can be read just before a baptism or a* brit mikvah, *immersion in the waters of life; it also makes for a wonderful opening invocation]*
How precious is your constant love, O God.
We take shelter under your wings.
We feast in the abundance of your house.
You gave us to drink from your stream of delights.
With you is the fountain of life.
In your light we are bathed in light.

Psalm 98
Sing out to God, all the earth,
Break forth and sing for joy.
Sing out to God with the harp,
And with voices full of joyous melody.
With trumpets and the sound of the horn sing out to God.
Let the sea roar in all its fullness,
The whole world and all its inhabitants,
Let the floods clap their hands,
And the mountains sing for joy
Before God and the nations.

Psalm 100

Serve the Lord with gladness
Make a joyful noise unto the Lord, in all lands far and wide.
Serve the Lord with gladness
Come before his presence with singing.
Know that the Lord is God.
It is he that has made us,
And not we ourselves;
We are his people,
And the sheep of his pasture.
Enter into his gates with thanksgiving,
And his courts with praise.
Be thankful unto him, and bless his name.
For the Lord is good, his mercy is everlasting;
And his truth endures
to all generations.

Isaiah 11

The shoot shall grow,
A twig shall sprout,
The spirit of the Lord shall alight upon these children.
A spirit of wisdom and insight,
A spirit of counsel and valor,
A spirit of devotion and reverence.
They shall sense the truth,
Shall judge the poor with equity,
And decide with justice for the lowly of the land.
Justice and faithfulness shall be theirs,
The wolf shall dwell with the lamb,
The leopard lie down with the kid,
The calf and the lion together,
And a little child shall lead them.

Genesis 21: 1–3, 5–6

The Lord was gracious to Sarah as he had said, and the Lord did for Sarah what he had promised. Sarah became pregnant and bore a son to Abraham in his old age, at the very time God had promised him. Abraham gave the name Isaac to the son Sarah bore him …. Abraham was a hundred years old when his son Isaac was born to him. Sarah said, "God has brought me laughter, and everyone who hears about this will laugh with me."

Mark 10: 13–14, 16

And they brought young children to him, that he should touch them: and his disciples rebuked those that brought them. But when Jesus saw it, he was much displeased, and said unto them, Suffer the little children come unto me, and forbid them not, for such is the kingdom of God …. Then he took them up in his arms, put his hands upon them, and blessed them.

Matthew 18: 1–3

At the same time came the disciples unto Jesus, saying, Who is the greatest in the kingdom of heaven? And Jesus called a little child unto him, and set him in the midst of them, and said, Verily I say unto you, unless you become as little children, you shall not enter into the kingdom of heaven.

Koran *[In Islamic baby naming ceremonies, the first Sura of the Koran is recited into the baby's ear, in Arabic or English or both.]*

In the Name of God, the Merciful Lord of Mercy. Praise be to God, the Lord of all Being, the Merciful Lord of Mercy, Master of the Day of Judgment. You alone we serve and to you alone we come for aid. Guide us in the straight path, the path of those whom you have blessed, not of those against who there is displeasure, not of those who have gone astray.

Blessings and Prayers

Blessings and prayers can be woven throughout the ceremony, including as an opening invocation after the welcoming words, a general blessing for the congregation, a blessing specifically for the baby, and a closing blessing.

Selection 1 is a gorgeous blessing that can be addressed to your baby alone or along with all the small children in your gathering. If you choose to include other children, simply change the first words of each line to read "Blessed be these children of God" and change "his" or "her" to "them." Your celebrant may place her hand on each young one's head as she recites a line. Sometimes it's fun to have the children line up facing the congregation in size order.

Selection 1, *author unknown*

Blessed be this child of God, whose very beginning is as our own and in whom we see infinite potential.

Blessed be this child of love, who reflects the love of God. May he feel a spirit of kinship with all creation.

Blessed be this child of wisdom, whose ever-expanding mind will touch the fount of knowing. May he learn to listen to the words and feelings of others, and to the voice of God in prayer, so that he will gain understanding.

Blessed be this child of eternity. May his path lead him to the highest pinnacles of life, love, joy and wisdom. May his life be long upon this earth. Amen.

Selection 2 [an Episcopal blessing]

Watch over this child, O Lord, as her days increase. Bless and guide her wherever she may be. Strengthen her when she stands, comfort her when she is sorrowful, raise her up should she fall, and in her heart let there be peace and understanding all the days of her life. Amen.

Selection 3 [by Rabbi Rami M. Shapiro]

We call unto the Source of Life
in thanksgiving for the wonder of this gift of life.
We are humbled by the blessings
and responsibilities of parenthood
and our participation in the miracle of creation.

May we learn to love without smothering.
May we learn to house without imprisoning.
May we learn to give without imposing.
May we learn to live today,
that yesterday and tomorrow
might find their own way in the world.

We give thanks to Life for the gift of life,
and stand in wonder
Before the awesome task of parenting that lies before us.
Blessed is the Way of Life
that makes parent rejoice with child.

We are humbled by the awesome power of this moment.
From our lives we have brought forth life.
Through our love we have fashioned a child of love.
May our child be a blessing to all he meets.
And may he count us among his blessings as well.

Selection 4 *["Our Wish For You," by Theresa Mary Grass]*
May you always see beauty in this world
And hear music every day.
May you know the touch of gentle hands
And walk the peaceful way.
May the words you speak be loving.
May laughter see you through.
May you be blessed with hope and joy.
These gifts we wish for you.

Selection 5
We pray for the life and well-being of this glorious child.
With his parents, we thank you for his entrance into this world.
We dedicate this child and this family to you and ask God's spirit to dwell
    here.
We pray for these parents and ask that they be filled with your spirit.
May they receive your love and strength with which to raise him, and your
    grace
and wisdom by which to guide this family now and forever. Amen.

Selection 6 *[a traditional blessing common to both Jews and Christians]*
May God bless and keep you.
May God's countenance shine upon you and be gracious unto you.
May God's presence be with you and grant you peace.

Selection 6 *[provided by Rabbi Joseph Gelberman]*
Beloved [child's name], as you go into the world, we call upon four powerful
    angels to assist you in life.
To your right shall walk the angel Gabriel who will give you strength.
To your left is Michael who shall protect you.
Behind you is Raphael who shall heal you.
And directly in front of you is Uriel, whose name means the Light of God.
    He will guide your way.

Selection 7 *[a Sufi blessing]*
May the blessing of God rest upon you,
May God's peace abide in you,
May God's presence illuminate your hearts
Now and forevermore.

Selection 8 *[by the Reverend Lynn James]*
[Child's name], may your life be filled with laughter.
May your heart be filled with song.
May your eyes be filled with beauty.
May your soul always know to Whom you belong. Amen.

Selection 9
[Child's name], may you always feel loved and cherished in your parents'
    home.
May you find in each sunrise a promise of a new beginning.
May no storm last so long as to shadow your spirit.
May you hear God's voice in the wind and in the sound of your own
    laughter.
May you see God's face in every person you meet, in every flower and in
    every living thing.
May you know that you are never alone, that you are guided by an eternal
    force.
May your days be good and long upon this earth. Amen.

Selection 10 *[by Molly Srode, adapted]*
    Bless [child's name], O God, that she may grow strong in body, mind
and spirit. May her lips speak the truth, may her heart find love, and may her
feet always walk in the way of peace. May her special gifts be recognized and
developed that she may know the joy of sharing them with others.

Selection 11 *[The Irish are famous for their blessings. This selection and the
four following are Irish in origin; a tender gesture might be to have an Irish
grandparent give the blessing.]*
    Welcome, little one! May strong arms hold you, caring hearts tend you,
and may love await you at every step.

Selection 12
    May God bless you with lucky stars above you, sunshine on your way,
many friends to love you, joy in work and play, laughter to outweigh each
care, in your heart a song, and gladness waiting everywhere all your whole
life long.

Selection 13
May the blessings of light be upon you,
Light without and light within.
And in all your comings and goings,
May you ever have a kindly greeting
From them you meet along the road.

Selection 14
May all the blessing of our Lord touch your life today.
May he send His angels to protect you on your way.
May sunshine and moonbeams dance over your head.
May good luck be with you wherever you go.
And may your blessings outnumber the shamrocks that grow.

Selection 15 *[St. Patrick's blessing]*
May you be blessed with the strength of heaven,
the light of the sun and the radiance of the moon,
the splendor of fire,
the speed of lightning,
the swiftness of wind,
the depth of the sea,
the stability of earth,
and the firmness of rock.

Selection 16 *[this invocation may be done in conjunction with a pouring of libation, an African tradition]*
All praise to God Almighty,
Praise to our African ancestors [or simply "our ancestors"] and roots.
God gave his power for the roots of the tree to spread its branches wide.
If a child does not know his roots, then he does not know his God.
Let the spirit of God and our ancestors bring us closer in unity.

Selection 17 *[adapted from a Navajo song]*
[Child's name], as you grow, may you walk in beauty.
Beauty before you.
Beauty behind you.
Beauty above and below you.
It is finished in beauty.
It is finished in beauty.

Selection 18 *[a Native American blessing]*
[Child's name], may you have the strength of eagle's wings, the faith and
   courage to fly to new heights, and the wisdom of the universe to carry
   you there.

Selection 19 *[Brachot 17a]*
May you live to see your world fulfilled,
May your destiny be for worlds still to come,
and may you trust in generations past and yet to be.
May your heart be filled with intuition
and your words be filled with insight.
May songs of praise ever be upon your tongue
and vision be on a straight path before you.
May your eyes shine with the light of holy words
and your face reflect the brightness of the heavens.
May your lips speak wisdom
and your fulfillment be in righteousness
even as you ever yearn to hear the words
of the Holy Ancient One of Old.

Selection 20 *[author unknown; a blessing often used in Brit Milah ceremonies]*
In every birth, blessed is the wonder.
In every creation, blessed is the new beginning.
In every child, blessed is life.
In every hope, blessed is the potential.
In every transition, blessed is the beginning.
In every existence, blessed are the possibilities.
In every love, blessed are the tears.
In every life, blessed is the love.

Selection 21,
   [Child's name], as your eyes are filled with wonder when you gaze at
the world, so, too, may you be filled with wonder at the everyday miracles
of life.

Selection 22 *[A Baby Blessing, by Welleran Pollarness; adapted]*

We hereby bless this baby, newly arrived, wishing for her all good things beyond our imaginings. May angels guide her flowering. May all she meet encourage her fragile mystery to bloom into radiant self.

Selection 23 *[a prayer for parents, by Rabbi Rami M. Shapiro]*

We are humbled by the awesome power of this moment.
From our lives we have brought forth life.
Through our love we have fashioned a child of love.
May our child be a blessing to all he meets.
And may he count us among his blessings as well.

Selection 24 *[for parents to read], author unknown*

Today we celebrate the blessing of our son. Beginning today we take on the responsibility of helping him as he grows to observe the commandments and live by values of righteousness and justice and to make this a better world for all.

As he begins his life, he is embarking on a great adventure that will include not only happiness and success, but possibly tragedy and sorrow. To live life in today's world will require faith, love, and courage. So God, we wish you would take our child by the hand and teach him what he must know to be the best he can be. Teach him, but gently. He will learn quickly enough that not all people are just, that not all are true. Teach him that for every scoundrel there is a hero; that for every enemy, there are countless friends.

Teach him the wonder of books; the joy of knowledge. Teach him to have faith in his own ideas, even if everyone else says they are foolish. Give him the strength to follow his own conscience.

And finally, bless him with courage and a sense of humor, so that he has the strength to withstand each trial of growth he must face.

Bless [child's name], dear God, and give him a wonderful life.

Selection 25 *[by Abraham Joshua Heschel; adapted]*

With every child born, a new experience enters the world. She encounters not only flowers and stars, mountains and walls, but a sublime expectation, a waiting for. Meaning is found in responding to the demand, meaning is found in sensing the demand.

May you remember that every deed counts, that every word has power, and that we can all do our share to redeem the world in spite of all the absurdities and all the frustrations and disappointments. Above all, remember to build a life as if it were a work of art.

You are unique, exceedingly precious, dear [child's name], not to be exchanged for anything else. No one will live your life for you, [child's name], no one will think your thoughts for you or dream your dreams.

Selection 26 *[by Rabbi Harry H. Epstein]*
May you be blessed beneath the wings of angels.
Be blessed with love, be blessed with peace.
May you always have ...
enough happiness to keep you sweet,
enough trials to keep you strong,
enough hope to keep you happy,
enough failure to keep you humble,
enough success to keep you eager,
enough friends to give you comfort,
enough wealth to meet your needs,
enough enthusiasm to look forward,
enough faith to banish depression,
enough determination to make each day better than yesterday.
And let us all say: Amen.

Selection 27 *[by Leonard Nimoy]*
May you be guided by the heavenly light,
May your dreams become solid and sound,
May your goals be well chosen and formed,
May your deeds be touched with decency and grace,
And above all, may you find the time to be kind.

Selection 28 *[a prayer for great-grandparents, by Eileen Chinnock]*
Dear Lord, the blessings that I've known,
Abundant love that you have shown
to watch my children grow and see
them reach their full maturity
and another blessing from above,
my children's children return my love.
And so, dear Lord, no more I ask
it's been a truly perfect past.
Whatever the future may hold in store,
my thanks, dear Lord,
I couldn't have asked for more.

Selection 29 *[by Chief Seattle; adapted]*
Teach your children what we have taught our children:
That the earth is our mother.
Whatever befalls the earth
befalls the sons and daughters of the earth.
This we know:
The earth does not belong to us, we belong to the earth.
All things are connected
like the blood, which unites one family.
Whatever befalls the earth
befalls the sons and daughters of the earth.
We did not weave the web of life,
we are merely a strand of it.
Whatever we do to the web,
we do to ourselves.

Selection 30 *[The Lord's Prayer, or the Our Father; one of the most significant prayers of the Christian tradition, finding its roots and theme in the Hebrew tradition. Interfaith couples may elect to say, "O God, who art in heaven ..."]*
Our Father, who art in heaven, hallowed be thy name.
Thy kingdom come, thy will be done, on earth as it is in heaven.
Give us this day our daily bread, and forgive us our trespasses
As we forgive those who have trespassed against us.
And lead us not into temptation, but deliver us from evil. Amen.

Selection 31 *[a Wiccan blessing]*
Blessings be upon this child.
Bring her ease and peace and grace.
Let her burdens fall away.
Let her keep untroubled peace.
Bring her every lovely truth.
Bring her every heart-whole charm.
Bless her in her pride and youth,
And protect her from all harm.

Selection 32 *[by Marian Wright Edelman]*
Dear God, I thank you for the gift of this child to raise, this life to share, this mind to help mold, this body to nurture, and this spirit to enrich. Let me never betray this child's trust, dampen this child's hope, or discourage this child's dreams. Help me, dear God, to help this precious child become all you

mean him to be. Let your grace and love fall on him like gentle breezes and give him inner strength and peace and patience for the journey ahead.

Selection 33 [the Prayer of the Faithful, a Catholic tradition]

[Celebrant] In the Catholic tradition, the prayer of the faithful is read at every ceremony. Please respond "Lord, hear our prayer" after each petition.

[Family member] That our families may be strengthened in a deeper bond of love, care, and unity through our commitment to these children.

[All] Lord, hear our prayer.

[Family member] That [father's name] and [mother's name] and the life of their child, [child's name], may be continuing examples of integrity, goodness, and justice.

[All] Lord, hear our prayer.

[Family member] That [child's name] may know the power and presence of love, affection, and tenderness.

[All] Lord, hear our prayer.

[Family member] For a continuing growth in understanding, openness, and unity among all people who share faith in God.

[All] Lord, hear our prayer.

Selection 34 [a Celtic blessing]

[Celebrant] Young one, listen to what I am about to say. Above you are the stars, below you is the earth, as time does pass, remember: Like the earth should your life be fertile, grounded in compassion. Like a star should your faith be constant, imbued with the light. Let the powers of the mind and of the intellect guide you. Let your faith in life and love keep you strong. Let the power of the strength of your dedication make you happy, productive, and whole.

Selection 35 [a blessing with the elements of nature, by Mark Belletini]

[Celebrant] We bless this child with the elements of our common being, with earth, air, fire, and water.

[Holding a handful of earth before the child] With earth, which is as solid as your given frame, my child, we bless you. Take good care of yourself as a body, be good to yourself, for you are a good gift.

[Blowing gently on the child's head] With air, which is as fluctuating as your given passion, my child, we bless you. You will know sorrow and joy, rage and contentment, resentment and ecstasy. Feel your passions, my child, for they are good gifts.

[Holding a lighted candle before the child's eyes] With fire, which is as illuminating as your given intelligence, my child, we bless you. Reason with care, test the world, think with care, for your mind is a good gift.

[Dipping fingers into warm water and touching them to the crown of the child's head] With water, which is as clear as your spirit, my child, we bless you. Grow in conscience, be rooted in good stories, grow spiritually, for spirit too is a good gift.

Selection 36 [a short, sweet blessing for the older sibling of the baby being named]
God, bless this child [sibling's name], brother of [baby's name]. May there be joy and laughter between brother and brother. May they be best of friends. May they cherish one another for all of their lives. Amen.

Selection 37 [a blessing of the home, in a home-based naming ceremony; the celebrant may sprinkle water or rose petals upon the floor]
Dear God, bless this home and all who live within her walls with your love. Peace be to them that enter and to them that depart. May this home be filled with the music of laughter, and the joy of shared time and spirit. May [child's father] and [mother] love each other as you love them. Strengthen their bond and commitment to one another. May they respect each other in all things. Let this marriage be a model to their children, family, and friends. Let these rooms be great halls of learning of your truth and grace.

Let your glory shine through these windows to their neighbors. May their kindness and consideration inspire others to love. So we bless the [family name] with length of days and years till the setting of the sun. Bless this family bountifully, dear God, and protect them from all harm. Amen.

RITUALS

Mankind has been creating and performing rituals since we were cave dwellers.

Rituals are significant if they have meaning for you, either personally, spiritually, religiously, or culturally. Then they are worth doing. In this section, you will find rituals based on various faith or cultural traditions, as well as universal versions that honor the child, grandparents, parents, siblings, and godparents. Some I have developed myself and to my knowledge you will find them nowhere else.

Candle Lighting

Fire has long been used to symbolize God's presence or spiritual illumination. At your ceremony, it is most appropriate to light a candle symbolizing the birth of your child, to honor his life and the light of his soul. You may use one large candle, representing the presence of God. Or you may first light two smaller candles, signifying the light of the parents' individual souls, and then a third for the newborn child. Siblings may light their own candles as well (with your help if they are young), representing their individual souls. In this way, you create a family of lights.

Selection 1

[Celebrant] [Mother's name] and [father's name], I ask you now to light a candle symbolic of [child's name]'s life and soul.

[Mother] Life is the first blessing.

[Father] Love is the second.

[Mother] Understanding is the third.

The parents jointly light a candle.

[Celebrant] Dear God, we thank you for the countless blessings you have given us. We thank you especially for the sacred joy and privilege of parenthood, which adds profound meaning and purpose to our existence.

[Parents] In the name of God and of generations before and after us, we welcome you, dear child, to the mystical union of souls on earth. We have awaited you. We rejoice that you are here.

Selection 2 *[by Rabbi Rami M. Shapiro]*

[Celebrant] [Child's full name] entered into our world on [date of birth].

The parents light a candle

[Parents] We are humbled by the awesome responsibility of this moment.

We are filled with joy and trembling as we contemplate the tasks that lie before us: Modeling love, teaching courage, instilling honesty, integrity and responsibility. May we come to embody the virtues we teach, and may our child see in us the values and behaviors we hope to see in him.

[Celebrant] We acknowledge this child as a living manifestation of God on earth. We dedicate him to God.

[Parents] We thank God for you, our precious child.

Selection 3 *[including a Masai prayer]*

[Celebrant] On [date of birth], [child's name] entered into this earthly kingdom. We rejoice that she is here. We now ask her parents to light a candle to symbolize this new light among us.

The parents jointly light a candle.

Receive this holy fire.

Make your lives like this fire.

A holy fire that is seen.

A life of God that is seen.

A life that darkness does not overcome.

May this light of God in you grow.

Light a fire that is worthy of your heads.

Light a fire that is worthy of your children.

Light a fire that is worthy of your fathers.

Light a fire that is worthy of your mothers.

Light a fire that is worthy of God.

Selection 4 *[appropriate if mother, father, or both are African American and the child is born near the time of Kwanzaa]*

[Celebrant] In honor of Kwanzaa, [mother's name] and [father's name] will light seven candles, representing the seven tenets of Kwanzaa: *umoja*—unity; *kujichagulia*—self-determination; *ujima*—collective responsibility; *ujamaa*—cooperative economics; *nia*—purpose; *kuumba*—creativity; and *imani*—faith.

[Mother's name] and [father's name], as you light these candles you affirm always to teach the light of these principles to your son [child's name] and embody these principles for your entire family and community.

Parents, now please light a candle symbolizing the light of your child's spirit.

[Mother and grandmothers] Beautiful one, beautiful one, welcome. *This refrain is often sung by African women at the birth of a child.*

Selection 5 *[from Kolot.com, adapted; may be used to form a circle of lighted candles with all members of the family and godparents]*

[Parents] We light this candle as a symbol of the collective sparks of life and love that is our family. As the flames join with one another, making one brighter and more lasting flame, so too do we come together. Much like the flames of this candle, when we share our love with each other our love is not

Since the day we heard about you we have not stopped praying for you.

Colossians 1:9

diminished, but enhanced, and within us the sparks of divinity burn even brighter.

Namings

The naming can take place on its own or in conjunction with a candle lighting.

In the Jewish tradition, it is customary to formally name the baby before the community and to call the generations—that is, to say aloud the names of parents and both sets of grandparents, thereby calling out the child's family lineage. Often, a Jewish child is given a Hebrew name.

A Muslim child is often given an Arabic name. Muslims conduct the "name-giving ceremony" seven days after the child's birth (seven is considered a mystical number in many traditions).

In Buddhism, a child is given a Dharma name. In the Sikh tradition, a name is chosen that begins with the first letter of a random reading from the Guru Granth Sahib (the Sikh Holy Book). In the Roman Catholic tradition, babies are often named after saints. Naming ceremonies are also rooted in Hindu, African, and various indigenous cultures.

Often, a child is named after a family member or a name is chosen for its meaning. Here is your chance to tell the world why you have given your child the name he or she bears.

Selection 1 *[a universal naming]*

[Parents] In our hearts, [child's name], your names will be Love, Joy, Hope, Goodness, Strength, and Faith. On this earth, you will be called [child's full name], beloved child of God.

The parents jointly light a candle representing the child's life and soul.

We rejoice in your presence. We thank God you are here.

Selection 2 *[in the Jewish tradition]*

The parents each light a candle from a large existing candle that represents God's illumination. Each smaller candle thus represents the light of their individual souls.

[Parents] [Child's name], love and joy are overflowing from our hearts. You have enriched our lives and we treasure the opportunity to benefit from lessons you will teach us as our lives unfold together in the years to come. We are grateful for God's gift of you, our most precious child.

Together they light a third candle.

This candle celebrates our child's emergence into this world on [date of birth]. We dedicate our child to God.

[Celebrant] What name do you give your child?

[Parents] [Child's name]

[Celebrant] What do you ask of God?

[Parents] To bless her.

[Celebrant] Is there anything you wish to tell us about the choice of this name?

The parents explain the significance of their child's name.

[Celebrant] It is with faith and a great promise of hope that we now name this child [name], daughter of [mother's name] and [father's name], granddaughter of [names of the four grandparents] and sister of [siblings' names].

[Parents] In the name of God and of generations before and after us, we welcome you, dear child, to the mystical union of souls on earth. We have awaited you. We rejoice that you are here.

Selection 3 *[in the Jewish tradition]*

[Celebrant] In keeping with tradition, by naming we honor those in the family who have passed on and perpetuate their names. By naming, we make familiar the unknown. To have a name is to announce one's uniqueness. To have a name is to belong to a family. To have a name is to give one honor. Who presents this baby for naming?

[Parents] We do.

[Celebrant] Almighty God, source of all life, we thank you for the countless blessings you have given us. We thank you especially for the sacred joy and privilege of parenthood, which adds profound meaning and purpose to our existence.

Is there anything you wish to tell us about the choice of this name?

The naming continues as in Selection 2.

Selection 4 *[in the Sufi tradition]*

[Celebrant] Sufism is the mystical sect of Islam. Its interfaith message is over 1,200 years old. There are many paths, but in the end they all lead to the One. God has many names, but there is only God. Now it is a Sufi tradition to formally name the child and present him to God.

Is there anything you wish to tell us about the choice of your child's name?

The parents explain the significance of the name they have chosen.

[Celebrant] It is with faith and great promise of hope that we now formally name this child [name].

It is also a Muslim tradition to put a bit of sugar on the baby's tongue and whisper prayers into his ear. How sweet! In conjunction with the naming, the celebrant may invite the parent to place the sweet substance on the baby's tongue and whisper prayers. In the Sufi tradition, the child's forehead is also marked symbolically by touch with the sign of the crescent moon and star.

Selection 5 [an African American naming]

In Africa, a baby naming takes place eight days after a child is born and in conjunction with the pouring of libations. Traditionally, the libation, corn wine, was contained in a small hollowed-out gourd and poured on the ground at the end. In an indoor ceremony it can be poured into a bowl or other appropriate vessel. Any wine will do.

[Celebrant or grandparent, while pouring the libation] Today we call upon our ancestors in blessing this child with the African tradition of pouring libations. In the words of Alice Walker: "To acknowledge our ancestors means we are aware that we did not make ourselves, that the line stretches all the way back, perhaps to God."

[Celebrant] All praise to God Almighty,

Praise to our [African] ancestors and roots.

God gave his power for the roots of the tree to spread its branches wide.

If a child does not know his roots, then he does not know his God.

Let the spirit of God and our ancestors bring us closer in unity.

[Celebrant, placing a tiny drop of the libation into the baby's mouth] We name you [child's name]. We welcome you into the world. We rejoice that you are here.

The congregation then shouts the child's name. After that, the parents may wrap the child in a beautiful African cloth.

Parents' Promises

The following two selections are rooted in Christian tradition. They can be tailored to individual needs.

Selection 1 [after each question from the celebrant, the parents respond "We do."]

[Celebrant] Do you promise to love [child's name] as God has loved you? Do you promise to teach her of the love of God, for God is love? Do you promise to see and honor [child's name] as soul, as that which is uniquely her? Do you promise to guide [child's name] and give her freedom to live the life that is her calling?

[Celebrant, bestowing blessings upon the parents' heads] May God's infinite love and strength be with you. Parents of [child's name], you are entrusted stewards of her soul.

Selection 2 *[after each question, the parents respond "We do" or "We will."]*

[Celebrant] [Parents' names], do you accept the obligation which is yours, to love and to nurture, to teach and to learn from this child who is in your care? Will you do all you can to help [child's name] be physically, emotionally, mentally, and spiritually strengthened to the best of your ability? Will you strive to embody, for [child's name] and each other, God's loving presence in your lives?

> **What the child sees, the child does. What the child does, the child is.**
>
> *Irish proverb*

[Celebrant, bestowing blessings upon the parents' heads] May God's infinite love and strength be with you. Parents of [child's name], you are entrusted stewards of her soul.

Selection 3 *[universal promises, by Andrea Alban Gosline, from Welcoming Ways]*

[Parents] We are your parents and we will care for you. We promise to reveal the adventure of life. We promise to love you unconditionally. We promise to learn from your challenges and inspirations. We promise to pay attention to each of your small moments. We promise to slow to your wonderful pace. We promise to embrace your hopes and dreams. We promise to open our hearts fully to your love. We promise to become a happy family.

Baptisms

Water has long been used in spiritual rituals as a symbol of life, rebirth, and purity.

In the interfaith baptisms I conduct, water represents an initiation, a welcoming into our world. We lovingly pour water over the child's head or we bathe him in a stream or shallow pool, as we invite him into our community as a child of God.

Use warm water if possible, for the baby's sake. A church may have a baptismal font, though many chapels do not. The water can simply be contained in a bowl held by the mother, symbolizing the giver of life, or the bowl can be placed on a ceremonial table. A separate table for the baptism water is an excellent idea, because everyone can gather around it. Sometimes a bowl possesses special significance—it may belong to Grandma or Great-Grandma, or it may have been a wedding gift to the baby's parents. The celebrant might silently bless the water before the ritual begins.

When Krishna's mother looked inside his mouth, she saw in his throat all the stars, all the cosmos, all of eternity and her own self.

Hindu story

Prior to the baptism, if a bowl of water is being used instead of a baptismal font, we sometimes pass the bowl along to immediate family members, or, if the gathering is intimate, to the entire congregation. Each person then places a hand over the water and silently says a prayer or personal blessing for the child, thus infusing the water with good wishes.

If it's summertime and your ceremony is being held by a shallow stream or other calm body of water, you may elect to bathe the baby completely. Older babies really seem to enjoy this. In some ceremonies I have done for one-year-olds, with the baptisms carried out near the end, the children simply stayed in their birthday suits splashing in the water for the remainder of the ceremony.

In the Christian tradition, the godparents customarily hold the baby. If you decide your child will be more comfortable in your arms, however, hold him yourself. The godparents then flank the parents on both sides.

Of course, do have a cloth or towel on hand to wipe the baby's forehead or dry her off completely.

Selection 1 *[an interfaith baptism for Christian/Jewish families; Psalm 36: 8-10 can be read just before a baptism or a* brit mikvah, *immersion in the waters of life]*

[Celebrant] How precious is your constant love, O God.

We take shelter under your wings.

We feast in the abundance of your house.

You gave us to drink from your stream of delights.

With you is the fountain of life.

In your light we are bathed in light.

[Celebrant, pouring water gently upon the baby's head] We baptize you as a child of God, as a child of light, and as a child of humanity.

Selection 2 *[the blessing of water]*

Water is the purest, clearest of liquids. In virtue of this, its natural character, it often symbolizes the nature of divine spirit. Water has a nourishing quality as well. All life comes from water. We ourselves are formed in the water of our mothers' wombs. Therefore, it is not surprising that water is used in many religious rituals around the world. We now use the gift of water to welcome this child into the world.

We bless you, [child's name], child of God.

Selection 3 *[a universal baptism, from Francis Thompson and William Blake]*

[Celebrant] Know you what it is to be a child? It is to have a spirit yet streaming from the waters of baptism; it is to believe in love, to believe in loveliness, to believe in belief; it is to be so little that the elves can reach to whisper in your ear; it is to turn pumpkins into coaches, and mice into horses, lowness into loftiness, and nothing into everything. For each child has a fairy godmother in his or her own soul. It is to live in a nutshell and count yourself the king or queen of infinite space. It is:

To see the world in a grain of sand,
And a heaven in a wildflower,
Hold infinity in the palm of your hand,
And eternity in an hour.

At the very dawn of creation, God used his spirit to breathe life into the waters, making them the wellspring of life. We now use the gift of water to welcome this child into this world.

[Celebrant, pouring water gently upon the baby's head] I baptize you, [child's name], as a child of God, as a child of light, and as a child of humanity.

Selection 4 *[a Christian baptism]*

[Celebrant] At the very dawn of creation, God used his spirit to breathe life into the waters, making them the wellspring of life. We now use the gift of water to welcome this child into this world. And so parents, I ask: Is it your will that your child be baptized in the faith of God's people as has been professed to you?

[Parents] Yes, it is.

[Celebrant] I baptize this child this day in the name of the Father, and of the Son, and of the Holy Spirit. Amen. Let us rejoice in this gift of new life. Blessed be God forever. For God has blessed and chosen this child as God's very own.

Selection 5 *[Christian baptism within a Christian-Jewish ceremony]*

[Celebrant] At the very dawn of creation, God used his spirit to breathe life into the waters, making them the wellspring of life. We now use the gift of water to welcome this child into the world and into our spiritual community, into this mystical union of souls on earth.

In the stories of creation and of the great flood, we see water as a symbol of life and death. Israel was led out of slavery through the Red Sea to be an image of God's holy people. Jesus walked into the waters of the Jordan and emerged anointed with Spirit.

And so parents, I ask you, is it your will that your child be baptized?

[Parents] Yes, it is.

[Celebrant] I baptize you this day in God's name, in the name of the Father, and of the Son, and of the Holy Spirit. Amen. Let us rejoice in the gift of this new life. Everyone please repeat after me: Blessed be God forever.

For God has blessed and chosen these children as God's very own. Amen.

Selection 6 *[universal baptism within a Christian-Muslim ceremony]*

[Celebrant] At the very dawn of creation Almighty God used his spirit to breathe life into the waters, making them the wellspring of life. Jesus, peace be upon him, walked into the waters of the River Jordan and emerged anointed, prepared to serve God. Muslims ritually bathe themselves with water before they pray. We therefore use the blessing of water to welcome this child into this world. In doing so, we dedicate him to God.

[Child's name], may God's illumination reside with you, now and forever. God's Peace be upon you.

Anointing

In this ritual, which is common in various traditions, the celebrant dabs the child with a spot of oil or other ingredient in a kind of blessing. The two following selections are anointings with lemon juice, honey, and wine. The third selection is an anointing with oil.

For versions one or two: Three separate small bowls should be in place at the table, one holding a bit of freshly squeezed lemon juice, the second, sugar water, and the third, wine. The celebrant can use a baby spoon to touch the child's lips with each substance. I prefer having the mother dip her little finger in each element, one at a time, and then bring her finger to the baby's mouth. Babies do enjoy sucking on their mothers' fingers! Parents have sometimes asked me if this ritual is safe for the child who is still only nursing or drinking formula. The amount of lemon juice, sugar water, and wine is miniscule, and in all the ceremonies I have led, no child has been hurt. Of course, if you are concerned, do discuss this with your pediatrician.

For the third selection: Have a few drops of oil on a small plate upon the ceremonial table or altar. Your celebrant may silently bless the oil as she begins the ritual. Then she anoints the baby's forehead, heart, hands, and feet. In an interfaith service, this is done with a simple touch—a dot or a dash, if you will. In a Christian-oriented ceremony, the child may be marked with the sign of the cross on his forehead. If you are of two faiths, the child may be marked with the symbol of both faiths upon his forehead.

Selection 1 *[by Rabbi Joseph Gelberman]*

[Celebrant] I anoint you with the juice of a lemon, for life will sometimes be sour for you. I anoint you with sugar (use sugar water here), for life will also be sweet for you. Lastly, I anoint you with a drop of wine, for whether life brings you bitterness or sweetness, it is up to you to make it joyful.

Selection 2 *[by Reverend Diane Berke]*

[Celebrant] There is a beautiful tradition in African villages to welcome a child into life. We first place a drop of lemon juice on the baby's lips. Life in this world sometimes contains experiences that are bitter. We pray that such experiences will be minimal in your life, [child's name], and that life's challenges will serve only to teach you that love is always with you and you are never alone.

Next, we place a drop of sugar on his lips, symbolizing the sweetness of life. May your life be rich in happiness and plentiful in blessings.

Finally, we place a drop of wine on his lips. Wine is a symbol of joy and divine love.

We pray that the joy and love you have awakened in us simply through your presence will flow back to you throughout your life, magnified and multiplied beyond measure. Amen.

Selection 3 *[an anointing with oil]*

[Celebrant] I now anoint you into our spiritual community of humanity, spirit made flesh.

The Blessing over the Wine

In Judaism, where there is wine, there is blessing. It can be a lovely touch if the cup used to contain the wine has special meaning for the couple or family—the kiddush cup used at the parents' wedding, for example, or one that belonged to a grandfather who has passed away, perhaps the child's namesake. Sometimes a new kiddush cup is purchased especially for the occasion, often by doting grandparents. In some interfaith services, we have used a plain silver goblet.

Of course, you can use kosher wine. Many a baby has been sanctified with Manischewitz!

In the following two selections, after the participants speak the words, the parents drink from the cup. Then each dips a finger into the cup and puts a touch of wine to the baby's lips. Often, we all drink—parents, grandparents, and myself!

Selection 1

[Father] At our wedding we drank together to celebrate our union. We drink again, for we have shared the greatest joy—that of participating in the creation of life.

[Mother] The sweet taste of wine is the symbol of the blessed fruit of our love. As we taste this wine, we sanctify our son and honor his name.

[Celebrant] You abound in blessings, Lord of the universe, source of all creation, who creates the fruit of the vine.

A grandfather may be called up to bestow a blessing in Hebrew. Or everyone can simply say "L'khayim—to life."

Baruch Atah Adonai, Elohenu Melech Ha'olem, Borey Peris Hagafen.

Selection 2 *[the grandfather or grandfathers are the participants]*

[Celebrant] The sweet taste of wine is the symbol of the blessed fruit of love. As we taste this wine, we sanctify [child's name] and honor him.

[Grandfather/s] Baruch Atah Adonai, Elohenu Melech Ha'olem, Borey Peris Hagafen. Blessed are you, Lord our God, King of the Universe, who creates the fruit of the vine.

Amen.

Selection 3 *[This and the following are two non-Jewish versions; at the conclusion, mother can dip her finger in the wine and place her finger on the baby's lips]*

[Celebrant] Throughout the ages, wine has been used for celebration. Often and among many people, wine has signified life, and drinking from a common cup has been the mark of deep sharing. May this cup of wine be a symbol of your lifelong communion of spirit, mind, and being. As the family drinks from this cup of wine, they undertake to share all that the future may bring. May whatever bitterness it contains be less bitter because you share it as a family. May all the sweetness that it holds be the sweeter because you share it as a family.

Selection 4 *[The parents each drink from individual cups, then pour some wine from each into a third cup, the Celtic cup, which the celebrant holds high, swirling the combined wine.]*

[Celebrant] The parents will now drink wine, symbolic of the cup of life. This drink is the embodiment of your families, your ancestors, and your bloodlines. It represents your lineage and symbolizes that which you are.

This wine now comes together in [child's name] name. For he symbolizes the merging of your lives, your love, your families, ancestors, and bloodlines. He also represents your greatest hopes.

The Pouring of Libations

This African ritual is a version of the blessing over the wine. Traditionally, corn wine is contained in a small, hollowed-out gourd, then poured on the ground. Ethiopian honey wine may especially appeal to the child, but any wine will do. The ritual works well in an outdoor ceremony. Indoors, the wine can just be poured from the gourd into a bowl or other appropriate vessel. The celebrant or a grandparent can perform the ritual, speaking the words and then placing a drop of wine upon the baby's lips at the blessing.

[Celebrant/grandparent] In Africa, the pouring of libations calls the blessings of the ancestors. In the words of Alice Walker, "To acknowledge our ancestors means we are aware that we did not make ourselves, that the line stretches all the way back, perhaps to God."

God bless you, [child's name]. We welcome you. We rejoice that you are here.

A Celtic Wiccan Ritual *[by J. M. Shedaker]*

[Celebrant] We ask God, family, and friends, and all of nature, to attend this rite and welcome this child into our community and to this earth.

Parents approach the altar with the baby.

[Celebrant] Who is this new traveler?

[Parents] [child's name]

[Celebrant] I bless you, [child's name], with the power of fire and air. *Touching the child's forehead with salt water.* I bless you, [child's name], by the power of earth and water.

Guide him in the ways of kindness and courage. Let him be valiant and wise. Give to him talents and appreciation for poetry, art, and music. Warm him through the long days of learning ahead.

Protect [child's name] with vigilance. Let him breathe in the fresh air of the forest and delight in the wind upon his face. Let him be as strong, free, and independent. Guide his footsteps. Protect him through the darkest of nights, and help him ponder the infinity of the starry sky.

One parent now holds the baby and faces him in each direction, beginning with east. Once the celebrant has completed the blessing for that direction, celebrant and parent walk slowly clockwise until facing the next direction, where they pause for the next statement.

[Celebrant] Hail east! Recognize this person [child's name]. Help him to soar in the limitless sky of thought and imagination. Send [child's name] gentle breezes to guide him on his path. Bless [child's name] with all the airborne powers of the east.

Hail south! Recognize this person [child's name]. Warm him, strengthen him. Send [child's name] light to help him prevail in the challenges that await him. Bless [child's name] with all the burning powers of the south.

Hail west! Recognize this person [child's name]. Help him to swim the deep seas of emotion and empathy. Send [child's name] cleansing waters to cleanse him of doubts and confusion. Bless [child's name] with all the flowing powers of the west.

Hail north! Recognize this person [child's name]. Help him to stand firm on Mother Earth. Send [child's name] rich soil to root in, and connect him with all that is. Bless [child's name] with all the solid powers of the north.

The Laying On of Hands

This is a simple and beautiful ritual that I have developed and that many of my couples ask me to perform. In the two versions described here, the celebrant—as she speaks the related words—gently places her hand in sequence over the baby's eyes, ears, mouth, head, and heart.

Selection 1
[Celebrant] [Child's name], may you see with God's eyes.
May you hear with God's ears.
May you speak with God's voice.
May your mind be filled with God's knowledge and wisdom.
May your heart be illuminated with God's compassion for your fellow man.
    Amen.

Selection 2
[Celebrant] [Child's name], may you be granted clarity of vision.
May you learn to hear the song of the universe.
May there be truth and kindness in your speech.

May your mind grow in knowledge and wisdom.
May your heart be illuminated with compassion for all humanity.

Honoring Grandparents

Grandparents typically love this ritual, one that I have developed.

In some ceremonies, we have been most fortunate to be able to honor also the great-grandparents who were in attendance. And in one ceremony, we acknowledged and blessed the parents' beloved adopted canine child. This was a dog they had found tied to a tree five years earlier, a creature, they said, "provided us with joy and happiness through our hardest of times." They hoped that their newborn daughter would "appreciate the value of having a special dog in her life and would come to love and care for all animals as if they were her children." The more heartfelt blessings, the merrier!

> **God could not be everywhere, so he invented mothers.**
>
> *Jewish saying*

I ask the grandparents to come forward, and then address them. Of course, they can remain seated, if that would be more comfortable.

[Celebrant] Beloved grandparents, this all began with you. Your fruit has multiplied. Just take a moment and look around at your beautiful family. We don't do this often enough. Let's take pause. Drink them all in.

God came through you to help create these wonderful human beings. There is nothing more beautiful or powerful on this earth than a loving family. Your grandchild will benefit from your wisdom. She will bask in the warmth of your unconditional love, the kind only a grandparent can give, the spoiling kind. That is your job. Grandparents hold a very special place in a child's heart. In the words of an unknown author: Nobody can do for little children what grandparents do. Grandparents sort of sprinkle stardust over the lives of children.

At this point, the celebrant can also honor grandparents who have passed on. One of the three quotes I present here can conclude her acknowledgment.

[Celebrant] At this time, we remember [child's name]'s grandparents [names] who cannot be with us physically, but who are here in spirit. They remain in our hearts. It is in their memory and in honor of all family members past and present that we offer this quote:

- [by Linda Hogan] Walking. I am listening to a deeper way.
  Suddenly, all my ancestors are behind me. Be Still. They Say.
  Watch and Listen. You are the result of the love of thousands.

- [by Alice Walker] To acknowledge our ancestors means we are aware that we did not make ourselves, that the line stretches all the way back, perhaps to God. The grace with which we embrace life, in spite of the pain, the sorrows, is always a measure of what has gone before.

- [by Albert Pine] What we do for ourselves dies with us, but what we do for others and the world remains and is immortal. [Names of grandparents], on this, your grandson/granddaughter's blessing day, we honor you. We thank you.

The Blessing from the Grandparents

This ritual may follow the above honoring of the grandparents. Sometimes the grandparents prepare in advance and may, in consultation with the parents, read one of the passages listed in our menu. For example, the blessing that begins "May you always have enough happiness to keep you sweet, enough trials to keep you strong" is extremely moving as the four grandparents come forward and, one by one, each places a right hand upon the child's head and reads one section.

Often, however, we just spontaneously ask them to come up to bestow a blessing. In this way, there is no time for anyone to be nervous—nor does anyone get too long-winded!

> Let your son pause to see there
> dancing in the currents
> a face much like your own
> a face soft yet strong enough
> to carry him home.
>
> *Linda Elena Opyr*

Grandparents love this ritual, as well. And many a one has thanked me at the conclusion of the ceremony for the opportunity to offer a blessing for the newest member of the family. At the same time—and this need hardly be pointed out—if you think there may be any discomfort in a grandparent, don't include it. One mother said to me in the questionnaire that while she absolutely did want to acknowledge her father, "I don't want to put him on the spot to have to say anything." She sensed that he was somewhat depressed and had been "a little fragile at recent holiday gatherings." So we simply gave thanks for his presence.

The first passage here extends the general invitation. The second is a scripted passage that a grandparent may prefer to read.

- [Celebrant] Now, grandparents, I am going to ask you to come forward, one at a time as I call your name, and gently place your hand on the baby's head. Please repeat the beginning after me and then finish the sentence in your own words. Speak from your heart. And please, be at peace. This is not a performance!

"God bless you, [child's name], I pray that ..."

- We are so excited to have a new grandchild who we can love and cherish. [Child's name] has captured our hearts and added so much joy to our lives. [Father's and mother's names], we wish for you to have from your children as much delight and happiness as both of you have given to your parents. May we have the pleasure of watching [child's name] grow and develop into the truly special person that we know she will become. We love you and hope all your dreams come true.

Appointing Godparents

You may prefer to refer to godparents as spiritual mentors or life mentors.

During the godparents' appointment, each is asked to present a spiritual gift to the child, one that is prepared in advance. This is a ritual I have developed, and it is one that has led to some marvelous moments. At times, a godparent has become a little nervous about the whole thing. He or she has called me before the naming ceremony to ask: What would be appropriate? Is this or that okay? Should I clear it with you? My response: There is no need to tell me, the officiant, ahead of time. Make a choice that comes from the heart. Let your gift, ideally, reflect your spirit—for what greater gift is there than the sharing of one's self? Let it reflect your joy at being part of this newcomer's world.

> **As we bring up our children, we have to remember that we are caretakers of the future. By improving their educations, we improve the future of mankind, the future of the world.**
>
> *Leo Tolstoy*

The honored baby may be unaware at the time. But as the years go on, a godparent's gift can inspire the child throughout his or her life.

In our completed ceremonies in Part III, you will find examples of gifts godparents presented to their godchildren. And there you will see why this is one of my favorite rituals. Share some of those examples with your appointed godparents, as inspiration for their own offerings. I can tell you from my experience with hundreds of families: give people a little room, a forum with which to express the love and beauty that lies within, and wonderful things emerge.

After they are appointed, I ask each godparent to present his or her gift and briefly explain its meaning. I then ask the godparents to come before me to receive a blessing and a simple laying on of hands. Sometimes I also anoint them.

In the following selections, you may wish to include the excerpt by Marianne Williamson, printed earlier here in the section on readings.

Selection 1

[Celebrant] Will the godparents please come forward?

You have been chosen by [parents' names] as spiritual mentors for [child's name]. They think most highly of you, trusting you with the spiritual care of their child. Children need other guides—ones they're not rebelling against!—for sometimes parents are just too close. You each have unique strengths, offerings they hope you will share with their child.

Godparents, inspire [child's name], be a friend to him, share yourselves with him. Allow him to dream great dreams. Nourish his soul. Help him discover his own majesty. Show him the wonders of the world. Let him know, really know, that he is never alone. And remember, sometimes all that is required is quiet listening.

Selection 2

[Celebrant] In times past, children were not the sole responsibility of the biological parents. This responsibility was shared in some ways by extended family and the community at large. As a reminder that children need many sources of support, the tradition of appointing spiritual mentors or godparents arose. These chosen people will have a special relationship with [child's name]. They will be there should he need someone outside the home to talk to. They will share experiences. They will be a neutral and loving third party should the family need help.

[Parent] [Names of the godparents], will you support us in the spiritual mentoring of our child? Will you be there to listen to him, and to help and advise him, if necessary?

[Godparents] We will.

Including Siblings

You may really want to consider including siblings, lest they feel left out or jealous. As mentioned earlier, a sibling can announce the baby's entrance at the beginning of the ceremony by ringing a handbell. Siblings can be involved in the candle-lighting ritual. In addition to or in place of those possibilities, you may wish to acknowledge siblings in one of the following special ways.

Selection 1 [*from* Weddings, Funerals, and Rites of Passage, *by Rev. Amy E. Long, editor, adapted*]

[Celebrant] Will [names of siblings] please come forward? This is a special day for you too. As a [big sister/ brother], you will teach [baby's name] many things. He already loves you very much and that love will only grow and grow. When a new baby comes home, the parents have to spend a lot of time feeding and taking care of the baby. Your mommy and daddy want

It is right that families should be contented in the home, that there should be children living there, vigorous and healthy as young olive trees.

Psalm 128, adapted

to thank you for your patience and understanding and your help. They want you to know how much they love you today and every day.

Selection 2 [*from* Weddings, Funerals, and Rites of Passage, *by Rev. Amy E. Long, editor, adapted*]

[Celebrant, placing her hand upon the child's head] God bless this child [sibling's name], brother [sister] of [baby's name]. May there be joy and laughter between them. May they be the best of friends. May they cherish one another for all of their lives. Amen.

Forming a Circle

When the ceremony is about to end, I often ask the immediate family members and the godparents to come forward and form a circle around the parents as they hold their baby, and join hands. If the gathering is intimate, I might have each of the participants first light small candles from a larger candle that has been burning throughout the service, representing God's illumination. We then have a circle of light.

In our completed ceremonies, you will find suggested words for the celebrant at this time. Here are some possibilities.

Selection 1

[Celebrant] Today, as we celebrate [child's name] and we welcome her into the [family name] family, into the community of their friends, and into the world, there is one thing we are certain of: The more this child is loved, the more she will grow as a human being, and the more she is loved, the more she will herself have love to give to others.

There is another thing: The more people this child feels connected to, the more people this child can ask questions of, the more people this child feels she can trust, the richer her growth will be.

So your presence here today is greatly appreciated, as your presence in [child's name]'s life in the future will be greatly appreciated. You each have unique gifts, offerings we hope you shall share with this child. It is said that it takes a village to raise a child. Look around you. You are looking at [child's name]'s village.

Selection 2

[Celebrant] A family is a circle of strength and love. With every birth and every union the circle grows. Every joy shared adds more love. Every crisis faced together makes the circle grow stronger.

[Parents] We give thanks for the gift of [child's name].

[Grandparents] We rejoice in this circle of family.

[Celebrant] We welcome her into our community.

Selection 3

[Celebrant] Please join hands, and with your hands your hearts. I will read a passage from *All My Relations*, by Mark Self.

Within my hand I hold my brother, father, grandfather, sister, mother, and grandmother.

Within my hand I hold the true spirit of giving.

Within my hand I hold knowledge of past and future.

Within my hand I hold the selflessness of sacrifice.

Within my hand I hold the hopes and prayers of life.

Within my hand I hold all my relations.

Look well at one another. You are all interconnected. This circle of family symbolizes the circle of life, and with each new birth the circle becomes stronger.

Selection 4 *[a children's circle; from Welcoming Ways by Andrea Alban Gosline; adapted]*

[Celebrant] May we ask all the children to come forward and form a circle around the parents and our baby of honor, [child's name]. Children, please hold hands. You will be [child's name]'s very first friends. So will you please repeat what I am about to say in your very loudest voices? "We welcome you, [child's name]. We are your first friends." Now cheer!

From the lips of children and infants you have ordained praise, O Lord.

Psalm 8:2

80

Closing Rituals

Most of these closing rituals I have personally developed. They are delightful finales.

Selection 1. Blowing bubbles

This ritual is so much fun, and it's a wonderful way to involve the other children who are present. It can follow the children's circle and their rousing cheer of welcome. If the ceremony is held outdoors and the child is a bit older than a newborn, your celebrant may invite all the children to blow bubbles around him.

[Celebrant] Bubbles make children giggle. Bubbles make children happy. Each bubble will represent a wish that [child's name]'s life will be filled with laughter and joy. We now invite all the children to blow bubbles gently for young [child's name]. Please be careful not to blow them too close to [child's name]. Blow them around him! Blow them high!

Selection 2. Sprinkling of rose petals

Indoors or outdoors, this is a delightful ritual. Mother holds the child on her lap, with Father right beside them. The celebrant begins the ritual and then all the immediate family members may participate. If your gathering is small in number, everyone can take part. At the end, you are left surrounded by rose petals, making for a wonderful photo opportunity.

[Celebrant] Rose petals represent life's sweet blessings, love, beauty, and poetry. We invite the immediate family members and godparents [we invite everyone] to gather a few rose petals from the baskets on the table, and then gently sprinkle them upon the baby along with your personal blessings and good wishes for [child's name] for the many years to come.

Selection 3. Holding baby high

This ritual is based on an African tradition, but of course anyone can do it, whether the child is a tiny baby or one year old. Older babies seem to enjoy the cheering.

[Celebrant] Our baby blessing is complete. The child has been blessed [named/baptized] and anointed. We now invite [child's father's name] to face the congregation and formally present his child to the community by holding her high. Upon his doing this, we invite you all to clap, cheer, and whoop! In this way, you all demonstrate your acceptance and your joy for this newest member among you.

Selection 4. *Ringing a bell*

I mentioned earlier that a delightful opening to a ceremony occurs when small children in the gathering process in sounding hand chimes. But a single bell can be rung at the beginning of the service or to signal the end, adding a dramatic note to the occasion. The ringing of a Tibetan bell is considered sacred. The following passage is a thoughtful one for the celebrant to read immediately before ringing:

[by Hazrat Inayat Khan] When one bell is rung, by the sound of that one bell other bells will also vibrate. So it is with the dancing of the soul; it produces its reaction, and that again will make other souls dance.

Selection 5. *The writing of blessings on papers*

An especially appropriate ritual when young children are present. People can tap into their creativity and have some fun as well. It is lovely to watch parents and children writing and drawing side by side, creating rainbows and other symbols of hope along with their written wishes for the littlest angel. Mom and dad of the honored child later usually put these into a scrapbook/keepsake for the child. You will need a basket or a bowl placed somewhere that is readily accessible to guests, and beside it many separate pieces of blank paper with markers and crayons nearby. I make mention of it during the ceremony, and people meander over to the area before, during, and after the event.

[Celebrant] Here you will find a basket and alongside it pieces of paper, colorful markers, and crayons. Before each of you leaves today, it is our hope that you will write your own personal blessing, a good wish, or a drawing for [child's name], for him to cherish over the many years to come. And please don't forget to sign it!

In the following section, I have reproduced several baby blessing ceremonies from among the hundreds I have conducted. You will see from these examples how all the pieces—answers to the questionnaire, selected readings, favorite rituals—can come together to create a mix-and-match, highly personalized occasion.

PART III

Mothers, Fathers, Babies

REAL LIFE STORIES, REAL LIFE CEREMONIES

Reading our real life stories will give you an idea on how to arrange and flow your own ceremony. But remember, the choices are yours. There is no right and wrong. Design the structure as you see fit, to include the parts and the people that speak to your heart.

In the interests of space and in order not to become overly repetitious, I have edited down and condensed portions of the ceremonies. Not every word or "stage direction" has been included. For example, I have not always described who should be holding the child at what point. But do not be overly concerned with this bit of orchestration. The answers usually come clear as your ceremony progresses. Another example: Although I don't always mention it here, I do announce to the assembled company what reading or other passage they are about to hear or what ritual they are about to witness. People like to be informed!

Your life is a message to your children.

Gandhi

In the interests of privacy, I have eliminated the last names of the families.

To convey some of the flavor of these very human gatherings, I begin with the story of Eddie and Kara and the baby naming we orchestrated for young Samuel James. I asked baby Sam's father to tell me something about the decisions he and Kara wrestled with as they contemplated what they wished to accomplish in welcoming their first child into the world.

His words, which open this account, and the descriptions of the ceremony that evolved bring to life the themes and issues at the core of *Bless This Child*: the need for two parents from different religious traditions to reach mutual agreement and understanding; the power of thoughtfully and lovingly balanced ceremonial elements to ease the discomfort of grandparents and older relatives; the wonderful opportunity in a ceremony like this to incorporate personal feelings, heartfelt gifts of the spirit, the funny or touching or surprising ritual that adds to the joy of the occasion.

Eddie, Kara, and Baby Sam

This young couple, both from the Midwest, met in college. They had created their wedding in large part by themselves, arranging for a rabbi and a priest to co-officiate. After moving to New York, they followed no particular religion. Once a baby was on the way, however, they wished to find not only a site for a naming ceremony, but a congregation in which to raise their child.

Eddie explains:

"My wife Kara and I were not novices when it came to thinking multireligiously. My very Catholic mother had converted to marry my very

Jewish father, and Kara's parents were from different backgrounds as well: Italian and Polish. So when we got hitched under a *chuppah* and signed our interfaith *ketubah*, witnessed by my cousin the Roman Catholic priest, we knew we had everything under control. Pride goes before the fall, right?

"We'll decide what religion the children will be before we set a date for the wedding ... before we get married ... before our first anniversary ... before we check the pregnancy test strip. For some reason, we were locked into the idea that our child had to follow only one of our religions.

"The problem was that we wanted to find somewhere to worship as a family. We checked them all out. There was the conservative synagogue up the street where we sat front and center with the rabbi's wife and where we were schmoozed with Manischewitz and *ruggelach*. Great, but the service was 95 percent in Hebrew. Kara doesn't know Hebrew. We tried two lovely Catholic churches, where I couldn't shake the feeling that Jesus's eyes were following me Mona-Lisa-like wherever I sat. Then we found it, I thought, a reformed Friday-night service with guitars and singing and circle dancing. I was sure this was our new spiritual home. It was just like Jewish summer camp. Then I looked over at Kara who was rolling her eyes and giggling.

"We took a long car ride. And on long car rides, during which neither of us can flee the room in a huff, the *big talks* happen. Someone said, 'No matter what we do, one of us is going to feel left out, and the other one is going to feel guilty.' Someone else said, 'Maybe there's another option.'

"We did a little Googling and found Reverend Susanna. We all met for breakfast, and she let us babble and fret and stammer about brises and baptisms and hurt feelings, and then she said something I won't forget: 'Don't say *instead of,* trying saying *in addition to.*' After that, everything was easier.

"I think my brother called it the 'bris-ening' (he also coined 'circumdecision'), and it took place on a bright Sunday morning in a small chapel at a Unitarian Universalist church in Manhattan. We handled the invite the way we did our interfaith wedding invite—here's what we're doing, everyone; we love you all and really hope you'll come.

"The task was to create a sacrament, a *simcha*, a ritual that would welcome Sam to his collective family and welcome Sam's family to the religious reality that we were defining for ourselves. Susanna helped us create a delicious recipe—a little bit of Judaism, a little bit of Catholicism, some UU to bind it, and some musical theater for flavor.

"The naming itself was very significant, of course. We went with Samuel James, Samuel being Kara's maternal grandfather's name and James being my maternal grandfather's name. The name itself was a bridge between our families that honored our past, gave each family an emotional stake in Sam, and created a really great, you're-in-trouble-mister name: 'Samuel James! What do you think you're doing?'

"What was wonderful and terrifying about the day was that most of the participants didn't know what to expect. But the amount of work we put into the ceremony really made it something vital and alive … and difficult, too. I sat up next to my wife and wept and watched the faces of our family members as they tried to understand what we were trying to create. Intellectually, it was pretty simple. We're raising Sam UU, and he'll visit for both Christmas and Passover. He'll hunt for Easter eggs in Chicago and the *afikomen* in Detroit. He'll get presents from Santa and open the door for Elijah.

"I'm talking about the bigger themes we were struggling to articulate on that day: we love you all, we know we are hurting some of you, this hurts us too, please love Sam. These weren't the familiar, comfortable faces that you see at a bris or a baptism, but we hadn't chosen a familiar, comfortable path."

The ceremony:

The Baby Naming Ceremony for Samuel James

Eddie was right. As the ceremony was about to start, tension was apparent in those gathered in the small chapel. The grandparents were already seated. There were no smiles. If one could read their thoughts, these traditionally oriented relatives were saying: "What's this going to be? What are our kids doing? I don't expect to like this."

Procession

In the entryway, Eddie and Kara held my hand and asked me to say a small prayer first. Then as classical music played, they walked down the aisle carrying little Sam, followed by the godparents and me.

And so we began.

Welcoming Words

[Susanna Macomb] Blessed are you who come here in God's name. On behalf of Eddie and Kara, I want to thank you all for being here.

When a baby enters our midst, face to face, hand to hand with this perfect creation, we cannot help but whisper to ourselves, "It's a miracle!" I often ask people to name a time in their lives when they felt closest to God. Inevitably those who are parents answer, "The moment my child was born." A child brings us back to who we really are before all the layers, the years, and the baggage accumulate. A child brings us back to innocence and glee, to the sheer joy of being alive. For a baby is so close to heaven. There is a beautiful story in the Kabbalah. Before a newborn enters the world, an angel presses her smallest finger upon the baby's lips and whispers: "Shhhh. Tell no one." The imprint upon our lips is a continual reminder of where we came.

A child has been born to Kara and Eddie, and they want to formally welcome him into the family and into the community at large with a ceremony that celebrates and honors both of their sacred traditions. Kara and Eddie said this to me: "It is important to us that our children learn about tolerance and appreciate differences in religion and cultures. We believe this will be an asset to them as they grow up."

Today before God, before parents, grandparents, godparents, family, and friends, we will bless and honor this newly arrived soul into our midst. Today we will give thanks to the Almighty for the gift of this healthy, precious child. For he is our future. He is our hope.

I am going to read Kara and Eddie's own words about their child:

"He is the most precious thing in the entire world. He is such a happy baby and he smiles all the time. He has been calm since minute one and is very good natured. He has long conversations of babble talk with us. We don't know what we did to receive the gift of a baby this good.

"We want him to have all the opportunities we had growing up and more. We wish that he has a childhood where he can play and laugh, challenges that he is able to overcome in order to become a man and enjoy the pleasure of having a child of his own. We want him to know that he is loved and supported in anything he chooses to do with his life, as we were. We also hope that the world he inherits is one of peace."

The Invocation

[Susanna] I will now read Psalm 100.
Serve the Lord with gladness
Make a joyful noise unto the Lord, in all lands far and wide.
Serve the Lord with gladness:
Come before his presence singing.
Know that the Lord is God.
It is he that has made us,
And not we ourselves:
We are his people,
And the sheep of his pasture.
Enter into his gates with thanksgiving,
And his courts with praise.

Be thankful unto him, and bless his name.
For the Lord is good: his mercy is everlasting;
And his truth endures
To all generations.

The Naming

[Susanna] In keeping with tradition, by naming we honor those in the family who have passed on and perpetuate their names. By naming, we make familiar the unknown. To have a name is to announce one's uniqueness. To have a name is to belong to a family. To have a name is to give honor.

Who presents this baby for a naming?

[Kara and Eddie] We do.

[Susanna] What do you ask of God?

[Kara and Eddie] To bless our child.

[Susanna] Almighty God, source of all life, we thank you for the countless blessings you have given us. We thank you especially for the sacred joy and privilege of parenthood, which adds profound meaning and purpose to our existence.

Is there anything you wish to tell us about the choice of this name?

[Kara and Eddie] Samuel was brave and ambitious. James was dignified and also ambitious. We hope he inherits both of these qualities.

[Susanna] It is with faith and great promise of hope that we now name this child Samuel James [last name], son of Kara and Eddie, grandson of Mary and Arthur [last name], grandson of Dwight and Sharon [last name], great-grandson of Sophie [last name], great-grandson of Bernice [last name].

At this time we also wish to acknowledge Sam's great-grandparents who are not with us physically, but who are here in spirit—James and Lucille [last name], Louis and Rebecca [last name], Samuel [last name], and Carl [last name]. We know they will act as Sam's personal angels, watching over him as he grows.

Blessings of the Grandparents

[Susanna] Beloved grandparents, your fruit has multiplied most beautifully. Just take a moment, pause, and look around you at your beautiful family. We don't do this often enough. Let's take pause. Drink them all in. You, by the grace of God, assisted in creating these wonderful human beings. I give you Emerson's definition of success: "Success is to leave this world a better place, by virtue of a kind word, a patch of garden, or by way of a child." You are a resounding success, for you have brought forth life. You have brought forth love. There is nothing more beautiful or more powerful than a loving and kind family.

Grandparents hold a very special place in a child's heart. Kara and Eddie wanted me to convey to you how much they love you and how important you are to them even though you are so far away. They want to include you in teaching Sam both of his beautiful traditions. It is most fitting on this day that we thank you. We honor you. We bless you. God is most pleased.

It is in your honor and in the honor of all their families, including their siblings, aunts, and uncles, that Kara and Eddie have asked me to read this verse on family:

Our family is a circle of strength and love.

With every birth and every union the circle grows.

Every joy shared adds more love,

Every crisis faced together

Makes the circle grow stronger.

Now I am going to call each grandparent forward by name, one at a time. When your name is called, please step forward and gently place your hand upon your grandchild's head and repeat after me, "God bless you, Sam. I pray that ..." Then finish the sentence using your own words. Speak from your heart. And please be at peace. This is not a performance!

The four grandparents, one by one, came up and gave their individual blessings, what each wished and prayed for baby Sam.

Watch over this child, O Lord, as his days increase. Bless and guide him wherever he may be. Strengthen him when he stands, comfort him when he is sorrowful, raise him up should he fall, and in his heart let there be peace and understanding all the days of his life. Amen.

Candle Lighting and the Honoring of Parents

[Susanna] Kara and Eddie, you have chosen the most difficult and yet most rewarding job in the world—parenthood. I often refer to it as the agony and the ecstasy. Being a parent, with all its joys and tribulations, will expand your capacity to love. It will strengthen and enhance your character. Everything Sam learns about love and how to be in the world will come from within his home. It is an awesome responsibility and an enormous blessing. If we really allowed ourselves to fully acknowledge, to fully let in, the amount of selfless devotion and plain hard work that it takes to be a parent, it would make our knees bend. It is apparent to anyone who has been in your presence for any length of time just how dedicated you are to little Samuel. You will no doubt be wonderful parents.

Each now kindly take a candle and light it, representing the light of your individual souls.

[Kara and Eddie] Samuel, love and joy are overflowing our hearts. You have enriched our lives and we treasure the opportunity to benefit from lessons you will teach us as our lives unfold together in the years to come. We are grateful for God's gift of you, our most precious child.

[Susanna] Now together please light the third candle.

[Kara and Eddie] This candle celebrates our child's emergence into this world. We dedicate our child to God.

[Susanna] In the name of God and of generations before and after us, we welcome you, young Samuel, to the mystical union of souls on earth.

[Kara and Eddie] We have awaited you. We rejoice that you are here.

[Susanna] Parents, do you promise to love Samuel as God loves you?

[Kara and Eddie] We do.

[Susanna] Will you teach him of the love of God, for God is love?

[Kara and Eddie] We will.

[Susanna] Do you promise to give him freedom to live the life that is his calling?

[Kara and Eddie] We do.

[Susanna] I am now going to ask you to read your words aloud.

I joked that when Sam became a teenager, he would remind his father of these words when he was grounded and couldn't borrow the car. Eddie was teary as he read.

[Eddie] To be a parent means to have the responsibilities to provide what my family needs and to know when to back off or stay out of the way. I don't want to smother Sam, in order to allow him to grow. I think that Kara is totally enamored with Sam and would do anything for him. She is calm with him and has an unlimited capacity to be with him.

[Kara] To be a parent means to nourish him and give him the ability to become a strong and loving individual and give back to society. We are his role models and should help him grow into the person he will become. I think Eddie is a great dad. He wants to make sure that he's doing the best for Sam. He wants to provide for his family and take care of them.

[Susanna] I would like to add that both Kara and Eddie told me they see God in Sam. Eddie and Kara, should life ever feel strained, please pull out these words to bring you back.

Now, Kara and Eddie have asked to read a very special lyric to Sam. It is a piece titled "Happiness," from the musical *You're a Good Man, Charlie Brown*, in which Kara and Eddie both performed when they were younger.

After the reading of "Happiness," I bestowed my blessing upon the parents.

May God's infinite love and strength be with you. Parents of Samuel James, you are entrusted stewards of his soul.

The Blessing of the Wine

[Susanna] Where there is wine, there is blessing, joy, and celebration. Eddie and Kara will now drink from the same kiddush cup of their wedding day.

[Eddie, holding the cup] At our wedding we drank together to celebrate our union. We drink again, for we have shared the greatest joy—that of participating in the creating of life.

[Kara, holding the cup] The sweet taste of wine is the symbol of the blessed fruit of our love. As we taste this wine we sanctify our son and honor his name.

[Susanna] Will Sam's grandfather, Arthur [last name], please come forward and give his blessing over the wine?

[Grandfather Arthur] Baruch Atah Adonai, Elohenu Melech Ha'olem, Borey Peris Hagafen.

[Susanna] You abound in blessings, Lord of the universe, source of all creation who creates the fruit of the vine.

Kara and Eddie then drank from the cup, after which each dipped a finger into the cup and put it to the lips of the baby.

[Susanna] We can now all say, L'khayim—to life!

With this prayer, I lay my hands gently over Sam's eyes, ears, mouth, head, and heart. Samuel James, may you see with God's eyes. May you hear with God's ears. May you speak with God's voice. May your mind grow in knowledge and wisdom. May your heart be illuminated with compassion for your fellow man.

Honoring the Godparents and Presenting Godparents' Gifts

[Susanna] Will the godparents please come forward?

Laura and Mark, you have been chosen by Kara and Eddie as godparents for their son Samuel. They think most highly of you, trusting you with the care of their child. Do you accept the responsibility of assisting in Sam's spiritual development?

[Godparents] We do.

[Susanna] As godparents, you will serve as spiritual mentors to this child. Sometimes his own parents will be just too close—particularly during those teenage years! Children *need* mentors, guides, other than their parents, people they aren't rebelling against. You each have unique gifts, offerings that Kara and Eddie hope you will share with your godson.

Laura, Kara told me that you were the maid of honor at their wedding. They tell me you are warm, loving, and beautiful, inside and out. They hope you will share your beauty, your inner spirit, with Sam. They hope that you will share your talents, including your beautiful singing voice.

Mark, you were the best man at Eddie and Kara's wedding. Here is what they said about you: A man of faith, you are centered and spiritual. True to yourself, you are unflinchingly honest without a drop of pretentiousness. They hope you will share your talents and spirit with your godson.

Godparents, will you please present your spiritual gifts to your godchild?

Laura, a professional singer, came front and center, looked right at Sam, and belted out a song with a voice worthy of the Broadway stage. She brought down the house. Sam was transfixed. Mark then stepped forward ("How am I supposed to follow that?" he said) and presented and described his gift, a book he'd made about all the Sams he could think of— historical Sams, funny Sams, family Sams, Dr. Seuss's Sam-I-Am, and more. "I hope the best qualities of all these," he said, "come forth in this new Sam, our Sam."

[Susanna] May God's infinite love and wisdom be with you, godparents of Samuel James.

The Anointing

[Susanna] The godparents may hold the child.

Samuel James [last name], I anoint you first with the juice of a lemon, for life will sometimes be sour for you, little one. I anoint you second with honey, for life will also be sweet for you, dear one. Lastly, I anoint you with a drop of wine, for whether life brings bitterness or sweetness, it is up to you to make it joyful.

[Godparents] We wish you long life and happiness. We trust you will be kind and compassionate. May you have success and good fortune. And may your life be one of love.

The Circle

[Susanna] Will all the family members and godparents form a circle around Kara, Eddie, and Sam?

They say it takes a village to raise a child. Well, you are looking at Sam's village!

Please hear me, family and godparents. Be a friend to Sam, share yourselves with him. There is no greater gift you can give. Allow him to dream great dreams. Nourish his soul. Help him discover his own majesty. Show him the wonders of this world, the marvels of this earth. Teach him to stand in awe at the mystery of life and to give thanks.

Help him to find faith in himself and to have faith in God. Help him find God within himself, in others, and in the world at large. Let him know, really know, that he is never alone. And remember, sometimes all that is required is quiet listening. Listen to his soul. Remember these famous words: Truly I tell you, unless you become like children, you will never enter the kingdom of heaven.

The Closing Blessing

[Susanna] May God bless you and keep you.
May God's countenance shine upon you and be gracious unto you.
May God's presence be with you and grant you peace. Amen.
Samuel James [last name], you have been named, blessed, and anointed.
Your godparents have been appointed.
We welcome you into our community.
As the music from You're a Good Man, Charlie Brown *played, our group left the chapel. Smiles abounded.*

In the reception room later, a grandmother—grandfather was deeply Catholic—came over to me and said, "I have to tell you something. My husband does not expound. And he just said this was one of the best days of his life, a terrific ceremony. And let me tell you, he's not the type to say anything like that!"

Young Sam was off to a fine start.

The Baby Welcoming Ceremony for Anya Becca

Bill and Meg had waited a long time for their child Anya, adopted as an infant. In the profile of themselves as prospective adoptive parents, they had written about their work running their own nursing agency delivering home health care to people living with cancer; about their wonderful, creative, supportive families; about their goofy dogs and cozy home; about holiday parties with numerous siblings, nieces, and nephews, and lots of music. They added at the end: "We strongly believe in open adoption and, should you choose us, can't wait to meet you to begin this journey together." It was from that profile that they were chosen by Dan and Jayla to be their baby Anya's parents. So began the "journey together."

In filling out the questionnaire (an "organic" form, Meg wrote, "it changes daily"), Bill and Meg sketched out their ideas for a very personal gathering. Anya's birth mother, Jayla, would be in attendance, as would *her* mother, Caryn (the baby's birth grandmother). Jayla was a "burgeoning Wiccan," Meg wrote, who had held a brief but beautiful Wiccan-styled ceremony for Anya while still in the hospital. There would be lots of infants and children at this naming ceremony. Could they all be blessed? Meg's family (and Meg herself) are very musical, and at least four songs would be sung. There would be no designated godparents, but all in attendance would serve as Anya's "godfamily." A beloved friend of Meg's, Anya's "fairy godmother," who had recently died would be honored.

Though Meg and Bill had each grown up in loving, solidly Catholic families, they planned to expose their daughter "to many religious beliefs, share our personal views as only one way to live, and support the path she chooses."

It all came together in a memorable event (written by me, but led by another officiant) in an open-air and glass chapel in the woods overlooking the Brandywine River in rural Pennsylvania.

The ceremony:

Procession and Opening Words

Anya Becca was held by her parents as they walked in while the ethereal music of "Morning Has Broken" filled the air. The beautiful stone altar held many objects of significance to the family and the day: the "croning cloak" that had belonged to Meg's dear friend Faith; a montage of photographs of Anya, to be presented later to her birth mother as a gift; a bowl for the baptism, rose petals floating on the water; stones collected from the trails near the family home, and more. The celebrant called all to a brief meditation, a communion with nature.

[Celebrant] Feel the energy of this place. Feel the power that is nature—the water, the sky, the trees, the earth beneath your feet. Become one with all of it. All nature is sacred. You are sacred.

Let go of your burdens. Exhale. Be fully present. Call forth your inner child.

Be at peace. Fill yourself with joy. Inhale. See with the eyes of a child.

If we could give you a gift, it would be this: At the end of this ceremony, you will hear the song that exists within the heart of a child, and know that this is the song of the universe in you, me, and all we see. With this lightness of being and an awareness of the interconnectedness of all things comes a sense of the sacred. In this knowing, life scintillates, its beauty unspeakable.

Reading and Welcoming Words

[Celebrant] We begin with the following reading:

This birth, this new life is not our first meeting, nor is this our first home. The welcome our hearts sing to you, oh round-faced one, has echoed down a thousand years. Here we are again, old friend, falling in love with you. Teach us your ways so that we may create ourselves anew. Teach us how to wonder and play, to greet the day with eyes so wide open that the world falls in. Teach us how to let go of everything that isn't love, oh infinite soul of our soul, one more time, so that we may know who we are.

[Celebrant] Welcome! Blessed are you who come here in joy! Make yourselves comfortable. Be relaxed and at peace.

Why are babies so magical? They are the closest things we have to heaven on earth. They represent pure joy, pure potential. They bring us back to a time when there was only hope, trust, and innocence. A child brings us back to who we really are, under all the layers of years, weathered experiences and judgments. A child brings us back to the kingdom of heaven within.

Today we have come together to welcome young Anya Becca and acknowledge her as divine manifestation, a living representative of God on earth. We celebrate the unique soul that she is. Today we give thanks for the gift of this precious child. We bless her and welcome her into our spiritual community, this mystical union of souls on earth. We pray for guidance for all those who will shape her life, all of you, her godfamily. You are the ones who will nurture her in realizing her full potential—her beauty, majesty, and grace—God's potential within her on this great path of the human being.

Honoring of Birth Parents, the Sharing of Wine, and a Blessing

Anya's birth mother, Jayla, was asked to come forward. The birth father, Dan, was unable to be at the ceremony.

Jayla, I give you Bill and Meg's own words: "Anya's birth parents are two exceptional young adults. Any time with them reveals that they are extremely caring people and that Anya's adoption placement was a supreme act of unselfish love."

Words can never express how profoundly grateful Bill and Meg are for the exceedingly precious gift of Anya Becca. They ask that you would honor them now by sharing with them the Celtic cup of friendship. Often and among many people, wine has signified life, and drinking from a common cup has been the mark of deep sharing. May this cup of wine be a symbol of your communion of spirit in your participation and celebration in the birth and growth of Anya.

The celebrant poured a small amount of wine into the celebratory cup and in turn, Jayla, Bill, and Meg drank a sip. Meg then took a drop on her little finger and placed it on the baby's lips.

[Celebrant, placing his hand upon the baby's head] We will now bestow a blessing selected by Bill and Meg, an adaptation of a Navajo lullaby.

The earth is your mother,
She holds you.
The sky is your father,
He protects you.
We are always together.
There never was a time when this was not so.
Blessed be.

[Celebrant] Jayla, on Anya Becca's blessing day, we honor you. We thank you and Dan for bringing forth the gift that is this child.

Bill and Meg then presented their gift, the beautiful photo montage, to Jayla with a hug and a kiss and a profound thank you.

The Parents' Words about Their Child

Here, the parents read the words they had written in answer to the questionnaire question, what does this child mean to you?

[Celebrant] Meg and Bill, would you please read your words to Anya Becca?

[Meg] Anya is amazing. To us, she means whole-heart opening. It's visceral. We can actually feel her in our hearts. She means long stretches of uninterrupted eye contact into her beautiful blues. She means we're collecting love songs about her. She means an extended family, through her birth families. She means we get to sing to her every day. A smile of recognition from her and the rest of the world falls away.

[Bill] She means that the dangerous low-hanging branches of the pine trees around the house have now, after fifteen years, been cut down to make her safer during thunderstorms. She means that we see the world through new eyes each day as we share her discovering with her. She means we now know that it's possible to live on far less sleep. She means that our cars are both victims of fender-benders caused by sleep deprivation, and our only response is to shrug and laugh.

[Meg] She means laughing and dancing and singing and acting goofy to entertain her and to be constantly entertained by her. She means "walking our talk" at a heightened level. She means we have to clean up our language—long overdue. She means we have the privilege of influencing the way another little person may interpret the world. She means a new teacher in our lives every day. She means we hold ourselves responsible for doing all we can to help her lead a happy life.

[Bill and Meg] We know that every moment of our lives was required to bring us to our joining with her. We are humbled, grateful and awestruck. We are regularly tearful with joy. And to quote Jim Reeves, "Miracles, it seems, really do come true." She means everything to us.

Ritual: A Song

[Celebrant] Music is prayer. It is the language of angels. We will now be graced with the gift of song.

Meg's family sang "Edelweiss" from The Sound of Music, *with a second melody written by Meg that blessed the baby and thanked God for her. "Anya loves this song," Meg wrote, "she beams!"*

Parents' Spiritual Promises and a Prayer

[Celebrant] In the Christian tradition, our parents will make spiritual promises to their child. Bill and Meg, as Anya Becca's parents, it is your responsibility to care for her with all that God has given you.

Do you promise to reveal the adventure of life?

Do you promise to love her unconditionally?

Do you promise to learn from her challenges and inspirations?

Do you promise to pay attention to each of her small moments?

Do you promise to slow to her wonderful pace?

Do you promise to embrace her hopes and dreams?

Do you promise to open your hearts fully to her love?

Do you promise to become a happy family?

After each question, the parents responded "We do." They then alternately read lines that spoke of what they dreamed of for their daughter, and ended with "A Prayer for a New Baby," by Anne Spring. The celebrant gave a brief blessing to the parents.

We wish for her:

A wide-open heart and mind.

A life full of happiness.

Peace.

Lots of music.

A childhood as wonderful as each of ours were.

True love.

We are grateful for this new being who is small in body yet great in soul, who has come into our midst as a gift.

May we be sensitive to the sacred as we nurture and learn from this child.

Give us patience.

Give us strength.

And grant us wisdom and love to help this child learn to sing her own song.

Honoring Those Who Have Gone Before

[Celebrant] Alice Walker wrote: "To acknowledge our ancestors means we are aware that we did not make ourselves, that the line stretches all the way back, perhaps to God. And the grace with which we embrace life, in spite of its pain and sorrows, is always a measure of what has gone before."

This is the portion of the ceremony that we dedicate to those who have gone before.

At this time we remember Patsy [last name], Anya's grandmother, who passed away twenty years ago. She is sorely missed today. She forever remains in the hearts of those who love her. She is one of Anya's closest angels watching over her as she grows. She communicates to her husband through music, so we have faith that she will communicate to her grandchild as well.

We also remember Faith [last name] who died on January 21, 2007. Faith used to say, "To have faith is to have wings." Fitting for someone who believed in fairies and appointed herself Anya's fairy godmother. Social advocate, pioneer, iconoclast, a celebrationist who loved to wear purple, high priestess, and a wearer of invisible wings, her cloak adorns our altar today. Her spirit resides in our hearts and in the hearts of all children. It is Meg and Bill's belief and fervent wish that Faith's radiant spirit will continue to inspire and watch over Anya from the other side of the veil.

We ask for a moment of silence to remember Patsy and Faith. Please remember as you knew them best, smiling and radiant.

Honoring Grandparents, the Grandparents' Blessings, and a Song

The celebrant called the grandparents forward with welcoming words and spoke of the special virtues of each of them, including the birth grandmother Caryn; she had written a note to the baby, "To Anya, who lives in many hearts." Each offered a blessing for the infant, in his or her own words, and then Meg's parents—from this very musical family!—sang the song "True Love" from the movie High Society, *a personal favorite.*

Universal Baptism and the Laying On of Hands

[Celebrant] We now use the gift of water to bless and welcome this child into the world, this mystical union of souls on earth. As we pass around the bowl, we ask that each of you place your hands above the water and infuse it with silent blessings for Anya.

As the celebrant poured water gently upon the baby's head three times:

We baptize you, Anya Becca [last name],

as a child of God,

as a child of light,

and as a child of humanity.

May you see with God's eyes. May you hear with God's ears. May you speak with God's voice. May your mind be filled with God's knowledge and wisdom. May your heart be illuminated with God's compassion for all of humanity. Amen.

Presenting the Godfamily's Gifts

Each of the family members and close friends in attendance—Anya's godfamily—had been asked by the parents to bring her the gift of a quality or virtue they would "hold" for her: love, humor, faith, and so on. Each gift would be represented by a small symbol—a stone, a feather, a flower—of that quality. Now, each member came forward and explained the significance of his or her gift, and then placed it in a lovely basket on the altar. These would be saved for Anya, gifts for a lifetime.

A Blessing for All the Children and Their Mothers

The celebrant asked all the children in the room to come forward with their mothers—the following day was Mother's Day. The youngsters formed a horizontal line in size order, with Anya in Meg's arms the last. Each mom stood behind her child or children with her hands on their shoulders; babies were carried. The celebrant walked in front of each child, oldest to youngest, placing a hand on each head and over his or her heart, while saying the following blessing.

"How shall I bless her, how shall this child be blessed?" asked the angel.

With a smile full of light,

Wide eyes to see

Each flower and bird and creature that lives,

And a heart that can feel for all that she sees.

"How shall I bless him, how shall this child be blessed?" asked the angel.

With feet that can dance on and on without end,
And a soul to remember all the melodies he hears,
With a hand to collect pretty shells by the sea,
And an ear that's attuned to all things great and small.
"How shall I bless her, how shall this child be blessed?" asked the angel.
We have blessed her with all in our power to give:
Songs and smiles and feet that can dance,
A gentle hand,
A heart that beats true,
And a soul that is filled with unbounding love.

Forming a Circle

[Celebrant] Will everyone please form a circle around Anya, Bill, and Meg? And will everyone please join hands and with your hands your hearts?

At this moon table,
We hold the chain of hands,
Mothers cradle babies reaching,
Fathers cradle mothers singing,
Taking their place in the tree of life.

Now, please, look around you. Look into the eyes of the person standing next to you. Acknowledge your own radiance and the radiance within each other. See with the eye of the heart. See how God sees.

The celebrant then read the passage from Marianne Williamson that ends with:

"We are born to make manifest the glory of God that is within us. It is not just in some of us, it's in everyone. And when we let our own light shine, we unconsciously give other people permission to do the same. As we are liberated from our own fear, our presence automatically liberates others."

In Meg's words, "And aren't we shining!"

We thank you for your participation in this circle of love and life. We are grateful for the gift of you. May the blessing of the Infinite go with you on your journey.

One More Song and Bubbles

The ceremony concluded with Meg's family singing "Long Time Sun," a blessing including the lyrics: "May the long time sun shine upon you. All love surround you. And the pure light within you ... guide your way on."

All the children sent baby Anya on her way with bubbles blowing. Hugs, kisses, and congratulations followed.

The Baby Naming Ceremony for Julia Lai Wing

About a month after a baby is born, usually on the new moon, it is customary for a Chinese family to host a delightful banquet known as the Red Egg and Ginger Party. Each guest takes home an egg—hard boiled and dyed red—for luck, and a piece of ginger.

So on a bright winter day in a huge Chinese banquet hall, a splendid dragon sculpture wrapping around the walls, baby Julia was welcomed. Father Carl, raised as a Catholic, and mother Mariann, who grew up, she wrote, "in a traditional Chinese household," wanted a ceremony that honored their families and their own inclinations toward Eastern philosophy and thought, particularly Taoism.

In Chinese tradition, a new baby is presented with a small jade-and-gold pendant, a "gift for life," and Julia was wearing her jade gift over her gown. Also traditionally, the baby is given a Chinese name by the paternal grandfather. In this case, Mari's father did the honors, and the baby had already been given her Chinese name, so we simply mentioned this during the opening remarks. In some ceremonies, the grandparents come forward to present the name as part of the calling of the generations and the honoring of grandparents, most important in Chinese culture.

Julia's parents wanted a ceremony that was not "too long or too extensive." The more ritualistic elements would be kept to a minimum. Grandparents would be thanked but not asked to come forward or speak. Basically, Mari wrote to me beforehand, saying, "We are not going to be doing anything except having the party." She added: "Be prepared to eat a lot!" And we all did.

The ceremony:

Welcoming Remarks

[Susanna] Einstein once stated that we could live life in one of two ways: One is as if nothing is a miracle, the other is as if everything is a miracle.

Behold the miracle of a child—Julia Lai Wing [last name].

Face to face with the birth of a child, this tiny perfect creation, even the cynic amongst us will whisper, "It's a miracle." It is that which is beyond words or explanation. It is that which brings awe.

Today we welcome and celebrate the emergence of this new soul. We acknowledge her as a unique manifestation of God on earth, therefore exceedingly precious beyond measure, not to be exchanged for anything or anyone else. A baby represents the future. She is our hope.

So the [last name] family formally and joyfully welcomes their child into their extended family and community—all of you—with the delightful Chinese tradition of a New Moon Red Egg and Ginger party. Red eggs have been distributed indicating new life, good fortune, happiness, harmony, and unity. If the child is a girl, an even number of eggs are given out; if a boy, an odd number. Ginger helps balance the yin and yang energy after giving birth.

Julia's parents chose her name because it was pretty. Its roots, however, are Latin, a nod to Carl's heritage. Julia means "youth" or "youthful." In this, we pray that Julia will always remain young at heart, like her mother. The baby of honor is also given a formal Chinese name, usually by the grandparents. Julia's maternal grandfather gave Julia her Chinese names: Lai, which means "dawn," and Wing, which means "pinnacle" or top. And so Julia represents the dawn, a new beginning, and we pray that she reaches the pinnacle of her potential, her inner majesty brought forth.

For our parents, having a baby is nothing less than mind blowing! Their lives have taken on new meaning, as well as a new level of exhaustion. Their love and patience have grown more than they could ever have imagined, and will continue to do so. I give you their own words.

Mariann wrote about her daughter: "In a private moment with Julia in the hospital, I thought, 'Oh my God, she's mine … all mine … wow!' I couldn't believe that she was part of me and part of Carl. I couldn't believe that she was here and she was already turning her head toward my voice, gazing at me lovingly when I held her, and that she had stopped crying when she felt my touch. I couldn't believe that she seemed to already love me after only really meeting a couple of days ago. Now, there are days when I wake up and I can hear people chattering on the street, birds chirping, the sun is shining through the curtains and it looks like the sky is going to be all blue, and I turn over and I see Julia sleeping soundly next to me and I am just thrilled and happy to be alive. I wish that Julia feels that way every day she wakes up. I don't care if she grows up to be the greatest musician like her dad wants her to be or a prominent behavior analyst for the autism community like I want her to be. I just want her to be happy and looking forward to every day of her life."

And Carl, this is what your wife wrote about you: "The first time I saw him holding our daughter and seeing how happy and in love he was with her, I just fell in love with him all over again. I do so each time I see her with him."

Carl, Mariann spoke of how incompetent she often felt in this new role during the first two weeks after Julia was born. (Join the club, Mariann!) She thought she was doing a terrible job. She wrote that on days when her hair is sticking out everywhere, when her eyes are bloodshot from sleep deprivation, you turn to her and say, "You're doing such an amazing job, I could never do this, you're a great mommy." She writes: "I love Carl more than I ever thought I could love him since we've had Julia."

Okay, now please kiss your wife!

Carl's words: "Having Julia has been a great experience. It's hard when she cries and nothing seems to satisfy her, but at the same time I always want to be with her. Coming home from work to Mari was always great, but coming home to my family is better. It's like falling in love again. When I can't be with her, I think about her all the time and wait for when I can see her again.

"I anticipate that watching her grow will be the best experience of my life. There are so many things that are measured by the passing of time and don't amount to anything. To have one that lasts so long and develops so much is profound. I know now that until you are a parent there is no way to prepare for how you will feel about it, and from the day she was born I became a father for the rest of my life whether I liked it or not! While that was a frightening prospect before her birth, those feelings disappeared quickly in the first weeks she was home. I am happy."

The Parents' Words about Their Child

[Susanna] When I asked our new parents what they dreamed or wished or hoped for their daughter, this is what they said.

She will be healthy and enjoy life and excel at anything she puts her mind to.

She will have a broad range of interests and always appreciate all that life has to offer.

She'll be influenced by all the best parts of her parents and learn from their mistakes and avoid their shortcomings.

She will have a great respect for life and never take anything for granted, and always love her family as much as they love her.

Mariann and Carl, you have chosen the most difficult and rewarding vocation in the world, parenthood. We, your spiritual community, thank you for bringing us the light that is Julia Lai Wing. (*I bowed to the parents as a sign of gratitude.*)

Julia is blessed to have you as her parents. The world needs more parents like you. And will everyone now give them a hand!

A Blessing

With my hand upon the child's head:
Blessings be upon this child;
Bring her ease and peace and grace.

103

Let her burdens fall away.
Let her keep untroubled peace.
Bring her every lovely truth.
Bring her every heart-whole charm.
Bless her in her pride and youth,
And protect her from all harm.

Honoring Grandparents

[Susanna] Beloved grandparents, this all began with you. Your fruit has multiplied, and multiplied beautifully. God came through you to help create these wonderful human beings. There is nothing, nothing more beautiful or more powerful on this earth than a loving family. Your granddaughter will benefit from your wisdom. Julia will bask in the warmth of your unconditional love, the kind only a grandparent can give, the spoiling kind. That is your function, and from your children, I hear that you are doing a great job! Grandparents hold a very special place in a child's heart. As someone once wrote: "Nobody can do for little children what grandparents do. Grandparents sort of sprinkle stardust over the lives of children." Grandparents, on your granddaughter's blessing day, we honor you.

Honoring Godparents and Presenting Gifts

[Susanna] Will the godparents please come forward?

In times past, children were not the sole responsibility of the biological parents. This responsibility was shared in some ways by extended family and the community at large. As a reminder that children need many sources of support, the tradition of appointing spiritual mentors or godparents arose. These chosen people will have a special relationship with the child. Laura and Jonathan, you have been chosen by Mariann and Carl as spiritual mentors for their child Julia. They think most highly of you, trusting you with the spiritual care of their daughter. Julia will need you, for children need other guides as sometimes parents are just too close.

I read to the guests some of the very affectionate words Mari and Carl had written about these dear friends. The godparents then presented their spiritual gifts and the parents, in turn, had small gifts for the godparents. Godfather Jonathan came forth with a live fig tree—a baby size, its root ball in a sack of earth—which he would plant in Julia's name. His Italian grandfather, he told us, grew a fig tree in his backyard and explained that the tree signified family and caring for those we love. Especially appropriate, as Carl, Julia's father, was one-half Italian.

[Susanna] Godparents, inspire Julia, be a friend to her, share yourselves with her. Allow her to dream great dreams. Nourish her soul. Help her discover her own majesty. Let her know that she is never alone. And remember, sometimes all that is required is quiet listening. Remember to take it light, as well. Have fun with her!

A Final Blessing and a Bell

[Susanna] Will everyone rise? Everyone please hold hands and with your hands your hearts.

Will you each fill yourselves with a personal blessing, a good wish for Julia for the many years to come? It is said that it takes a village to raise a child. Look around. You are Julia's village. You are her angels on earth.

Ladies and gentlemen, the rite is done, the child is blessed, the godparents have been appointed. We thank you for your presence today. You are a gift in this family's life, as Julia is a gift. These are gifts for which we are most grateful.

Years ago, I read the following words and rang this Tibetan bell at the beginning of Carl and Mariann's wedding ceremony. Today I will read these same words and ring this bell to end Julia's baby blessing ceremony. Today this bell also serves as the dinner bell!

"When one bell is rung, by the sound of that one bell other bells will also vibrate. So it is with the dancing of the soul. It produces its reaction and that again will make other souls dance."

Neither parent practiced any particular religion, Mariann had explained while we designed the occasion, and they preferred not to include "anything resembling a christening." Her husband's family believed such a ritual should be performed only in a Catholic church. Yet at the conclusion of our naming ceremony, as the lively party got underway, Julia's paternal grandmother asked quietly if the baby could be baptized. So we conducted a private, last-minute baptism to one side. It spoke to the power of an interfaith, intercultural, personalized ceremony, rooted in love, to bring all together.

The Baby Naming Ceremony for Aiden Jonah

On a summer day at a lovely home in the country, friends and family of Gene and Robert gathered to welcome their baby Aiden.

These two doting dads, a gay couple, had pulled out all the stops to ensure a memorable occasion. A tent where the ceremony would be held had been set up over the lawn. One of Aiden's fathers cooked all the food, a splendid repast. The other made a video of the whole process that had led to this day: meeting the surrogate mother, their son's birth, grandparents holding the newest member of the family, all interspersed with sentences from their selected readings—a twenty-minute show, complete with music, playing on a giant TV in the house living room!

Robbie and Gene had carefully chosen a wide assortment of elements that would honor and acknowledge their Catholic/Jewish union. The family processed in, followed by the godparents, to the music of John Lennon's "Beautiful Boy."

The ceremony:

Welcoming Remarks

[Susanna] Before we begin, I am going to ask each of you to take a deep breath. It may help if you close your eyes. With each breath, let go of all the stress of this past week. Let go of all the pending problems in your life. Simply be. Now call upon the source of all life, the divine within. Ask God to fill every cell of your being with grace—pure, radiant, scintillating light. Let there be peace in your soul. Here is a short cut: Fill yourselves with the love you have for the people you care for most. Fill yourselves with the love you have for Robbie and Gene. Fill yourselves with the love you have for baby Aiden Jonah. God is love. And it is in loving one another that we know God. For today's ceremony, I also ask that we fill ourselves with the magic and the innocence that is a child. Today, let us see with the eyes of a child, eyes filled with wonder and innocence.

Please open your eyes now.

Shalom! Welcome! The physicist Albert Einstein once said that we can live life in one of two ways: One as if nothing is a miracle, the other as if everything is a miracle. Walt Whitman saw every cubic foot around him "swarming with miracles." Today, we are going to ask you to stand with us in a little bit of awe and a whole lot of gratitude at the miracle of a child. If we want to feel truly alive, we must learn to see the miraculous in the everyday, as in this baby before us. There is a lot of God in a baby.

Robbie and Gene had written at length in the questionnaire about their devotion to their new son, and I read many of their statements to the guests. Here are just a few:

Gene wrote: "I didn't know what pain meant until I felt his pain. I didn't know what happiness was until I saw him smile and heard his laugh. Nothing else matters when I hold him in my arms! I feel an awesome sense of responsibility for another human being. It is overwhelming at times but so incredibly rewarding. When Aiden looks at me, really looks at me with this abundant trust in his eyes, my heart skips a beat … and I feel that I can do anything for him."

Robbie wrote: "He is the most extraordinary gift God has brought to us. My father always said that I would never understand true unconditional love until I experienced the love for my child. I now know what he meant. My son is the most important thing in my life. My heart feels like it lives outside my body. This is the only way I can explain my true feelings. My brother put it perfectly when he said that I was no longer number one! Without hesitation, I have taken the backseat to my amazing son. He comes before anything."

So this is big! A day to celebrate! Today we are gathered together to acknowledge Aiden Jonah [last name] as the radiant soul that he is. Today we welcome him into our spiritual community, with profound and prayerful gratitude.

I ended the welcoming remarks by observing that the ceremony to follow was carefully chosen by Aiden's parents to celebrate their Jewish and Christian traditions, in a reflection of how their child will be raised—with tolerance, respect, and understanding. No one is excluded. Everyone is welcomed and honored.

A Blessing and Anointing

[Susanna] Aiden *(with my hands on his eyes),* may you always see beauty in this world *(hands on his ears)* and hear music every day.

(Hands on his hands) May you know the touch of gentle hands *(hands on his feet)* and walk the peaceful way.

(Hands on his mouth) May the words you speak be loving. May laughter see you through.

(Hands on his heart) May you be blessed with hope and joy. *(Hands on his head)* These gifts we wish for you. Amen.

Aiden was anointed with a drop of oil on his head, heart, hands, and feet.

The Naming and the Calling of Generations

[Susanna] In keeping with Jewish tradition, by naming we honor those in the family who have passed on and perpetuate their names. By naming, we make familiar the unknown. To have a name is to announce one's uniqueness. To have a name is to belong to a family. To have a name is to give one honor. Who presents this baby for naming?

[Parents] We do.

[Susanna] Almighty God, source of all life, we thank you for the countless blessings you have given us. We thank you especially for the sacred joy and privilege of parenthood, which adds profound meaning and purpose to our existence.

[Parents] We are humbled by the awesome power of this moment. From our lives we have brought forth life. Through our love we have fashioned a child of love. May our child be a blessing to all he meets. And may he count us among his blessings as well.

[Susanna] Is there anything you wish to tell us about the choice of this name?

[Robbie] Aiden's middle name, Jonah, was given in honor of his grandma, who is in heaven and her spirit lives on. I had a very special relationship with my mother and often joked and called her Jonah. Her real name was Joanie. She was the most devoted, loyal, loving mother and friend. She's undoubtedly our son's guardian angel and watches over Aiden and will do so for the rest of his life.

[Gene] We give our son the Hebrew name Haim, which means life, and which belonged to Aiden's great-grandfather, my father Vladimir's father. We pray that Aiden will be full of life and blessed with a good life.

[Susanna] It is with faith and a great promise of hope that we now name this child Aiden Jonah Haim [last name], son of Robert [last name] and Gene [last name], grandson of Matthew and Joan [last name], grandson of Vladimir and Raisa [last name].

[Parents] In the name of God and of generations before and after us, we welcome you, dear child, to the mystical union of souls on earth. We have awaited you. We rejoice that you are here.

The Parents' Prayer

Gene and Robbie alternated reading a line each.

Aiden, if there could be only one thing in life for us to teach you, we would teach you to love.

To respect others so that you may find respect in yourself.

To learn the value of giving, so that if ever there comes a time in your life that someone really needs, you will give.

To act in a manner that you would wish to be treated, to be proud of yourself.

To laugh and smile as much as you can, in order to help bring joy back into this world.

To have faith in others, to be understanding, to stand tall in the world, and to learn to depend on yourself.

To take from this earth only those things which you really need, so there will be enough for others.

To not depend on money or material things for your happiness, but to learn to appreciate the people who love you, the simple beauty that God gave you, and to find peace and security within yourself.

To you, our child, we hope we will teach all these things, for they are love. Amen.

Candle Lighting and a Masai Prayer

[Susanna] On January 20, 2009, Aiden Jonah Haim [last name] entered into this earthly kingdom. We now ask his parents to light a candle to symbolize this new light among us.

[Parents] Receive this holy fire.
Make your lives like this fire.
A holy fire that is seen.
A life of God that is seen.
A life that darkness does not overcome.
May this light of God in you grow.
Light a fire that is worthy of your heads.
Light a fire that is worthy of your children.
Light a fire that is worthy of your fathers.
Light a fire that is worthy of your mothers.
Light a fire that is worthy of God.

Blessing and Anointing of the Parents

Robbie and Gene were clearly such caring parents. I spoke of the challenges and delights ahead on their path and thanked them on behalf of their family and friends for bringing us Aiden, before anointing them and offering this blessing:

[Susanna] May God grant you the love, wisdom, strength, and compassion needed in this role. You are temporary stewards of Aiden's spirit.

Christian Baptism

[Susanna] In the stories of creation and of the great flood, we see water as a symbol of life. Israel was led out of slavery through the Red Sea to be an image of God's holy people. Rabbi Jesus walked into the waters of the Jordan and emerged anointed with Spirit. We now use the gift of water to welcome this child into the world and into our spiritual community. And so parents, I ask you: Is it your will that your child be baptized?

[Parents] Yes, it is.

[Susanna] Aiden, I baptize you this day in God's name, in the name of the Father, and of the Son, and of the Holy Spirit. Amen. Let us rejoice in the gift of this new life. Everyone please repeat after me: Blessed be God forever.

[All] Blessed be God forever.

[Susanna] For God has blessed and chosen this child as God's very own. Amen.

The Blessing over the Wine in the Jewish Tradition

[Robbie] We drink for we have shared the greatest joy, that of participating in the creation of life.

[Gene] The sweet taste of wine is the symbol of the blessed fruit of our love. As we taste this wine we sanctify our son and honor his name.

[Susanna] You abound in blessings, Lord of the universe, source of all creation, who creates the fruit of the vine.

We now invite Grandfather Vladimir to bestow blessing over the wine in Hebrew.

[Grandfather] Baruch Atah Adonai, Elohenu Melech Ha'olem, Borey Peris Hagafen.

The wine was passed from Grandfather Vladimir to his son, Gene, and then to Robbie. Gene put a drop of wine upon Aiden's lips, and then Susanna had a sip of wine.

[Susanna] L'khayim! To life!

Honoring Grandparents

[Susanna] I now call forth the grandparents, who I hear are utterly in love with their new grandson. Grandparents, I want to read your children's words:

Gene wrote: "My parents taught me to be independent. They taught me discipline in life. They gave me confidence in their unconditional love and support."

Robbie wrote: "My father said that I should love Aiden as much as I was loved as a child, and Aiden will turn out just fine."

After my words of thanks and appreciation, the three grandparents came up one by one and offered a spontaneous blessing for their grandson in their own words. We had a moment of quiet to remember Robbie's late mother, his devoted Joanie.

[Susanna] In her honor, we dedicate this quote by Linda Hogan, a Native American poet, novelist, and Pulitzer Prize winner:

"Walking. I am listening to a deeper way. Suddenly, all my ancestors are behind me. Be Still. They Say. Watch and Listen. You are the result of the love of thousands."

Honoring and Anointing Godparents and Presenting Gifts

Young Aiden had three godparents, Robbie and Gene's closest friends. One of them, a woman who was Robbie's dear friend for twenty-five years, was unable to attend the ceremony. Our two others were a Christian godfather and a Jewish godfather. Among my words to them was the quotation written by Marianne Williamson, one I often offer to those who will teach and guide children. These were the godparents' spiritual gifts: a Christian reliquary, to be placed on Aiden's crib, to protect him, and a chain containing a specially designed combination of Christian and Jewish symbols, a gift of special meaning, as it had always been worn by the godparent himself.

[Susanna] Godmother Jennifer has sent this message, which I will read in her absence: "Aiden, may you be blessed with the strength of heaven, the light of the sun and the radiance of the moon, the splendor of fire, the speed of lightning, the swiftness of wind, the depth of the sea, the stability of earth, and the firmness of rock."

I anoint you godparents of Aiden Jonah Haim [last name]. May God grant you the love, wisdom, and compassion you will need in this role. Amen. And thank you.

A Final Blessing

[Susanna] Aiden, may you always feel loved and cherished in your parents' home.

May you know that each sunrise is a promise of a new beginning.

May no storm last so long as to shadow your spirit.

May you hear God's voice in the wind and in the sound of your own laughter.

May you see God's face in every person you meet, in every flower and in every living thing.

May you know that you are never alone, that you are guided by an eternal force.

May your days be good and long upon this earth. Amen.

Forming a Circle and Blowing Bubbles

[Susanna] Parents, please bring your child in the center of this circle. Family and friends, make a circle around our family of honor and hold hands.

Today as we celebrate Aiden and welcome him into his family and into the community of their friends and into the world, of this we are certain:

The more this child is loved, the more he will grow as a human being, and the more he is loved, the more he will himself have love to give to others.

The more people this child feels connected to, the more people this child can ask questions of, the more people this child feels he can trust, the richer his growth will be.

So your presence here today is greatly appreciated, as your presence in Aiden's life in the future will be greatly appreciated. You each have unique gifts, offerings we hope you will share with this child. It is said that it takes a village to raise a child. Well, look around you, you are looking at Aiden's village.

Now, some bubbles! Bubbles make children giggle. Bubbles make children happy. We now invite all the children to gently blow bubbles for young Aiden. Each bubble will represent a wish that Aiden's life be filled with laughter and joy. And please be careful, children, not to blow them too close to Aiden's face. Blow them around him! Blow them high!

The rite is done. The child has been blessed, named, baptized, and anointed. He has been formally welcomed into this mystical community of souls on earth. His godparents have been appointed. I want to thank Aidan's family for the privilege of conducting his blessing ceremony. It has indeed been a privilege. You are the gift. A gift for which I am most grateful.

The ringing of this bell indicates the end of the ceremony, and also serves as the brunch bell!

Louis Armstrong's "What a Wonderful World" played. The festivities continued throughout a splendid day.

The Baby Naming Ceremony for Benjamin Simon

In the small, exquisite St. Paul's Chapel on the campus of Columbia University in New York, we celebrated baby Benjamin. His mother grew up in the Greek Orthodox tradition and father in the Jewish tradition, and some years earlier I had performed their wedding ceremony at the chapel. Guests at Benjamin's ceremony were treated to the marvelous sounds of a piano played by a professional pianist and a good friend of mother Nancy's, and this was a carefully choreographed, spirited medley: show tunes from *Pippin*,

Les Miserables, Phantom of the Opera, The Little Mermaid, Hair, and others, plus some Leonard Bernstein, some Beatles, and, appropriately, George M. Cohan's "Yankee Doodle Dandy."

The ceremony:

Welcoming Remarks

As part of my greeting to the guests, I included some of the parents' questionnaire comments:

[Susanna] It is my experience that children come into the world with a particular spirit. Here is what our parents say about Benjamin:

"Looking back, it seems like Benjamin's personality existed before he was born, from the time he decided that he would enter this world on July 4, when our country was celebrating. He is a firecracker. He lights up a room, first looking at you intently, and then revealing his smile. He even gets greetings from strangers and we've met all kinds of people due to him. He's always curious, moving, grabbing, smiling, making noises, laughing, looking at what's going on. He likes to be in the center of it all."

Our parents also tell me that they take Benjamin everywhere they go—beginning with a two-mile walk the day they brought him home from the hospital at only two days old. Benjamin has gone along with his parents hiking, snow shoeing, playing tennis, swimming, visiting with friends; he's gone to restaurants, basketball games, and parties. And he seems to take it all in stride.

Benjamin is a very *present* soul.

Today, before God, family, and friends, we will bless and honor this newly arrived soul into our midst. Today we give thanks for the gift of this healthy, precious child. For he is the future. He is our hope. May young Benjamin lead our way.

A Blessing and Anointing

[Susanna] Benjamin, may your life be filled with laughter (*as I placed my hands gently on his mouth*), may your heart be filled with song (*hands on heart*), may your eyes be filled with beauty (*hands on eyes*), may your soul always know to whom you belong (*hands on head*).

A Reading

[Susanna] Our first reading, selected by our parents, is from *The Prophet* by Kahlil Gibran, read by Benjamin's mother, Nancy. I believe this is one of the most enlightened pieces—if not the most enlightened—ever written about children.

[Nancy] "And a woman who held a babe against her bosom said, Speak to us of Children. And he said: Your children are not your children. They are the sons and daughters of Life's longing for itself. They come through you but not from you. And though they are with you yet they belong not to you.

"You may give them your love but not your thoughts, for they have their own thoughts. You may house their bodies but not their souls, for their souls dwell in the house of tomorrow, which you cannot visit, not even in your dreams.

"You may strive to be like them, but seek not to make them like you. For life goes not backward nor tarries with yesterday.

"You are the bows from which your children as living arrows are sent forth. The archer sees the mark upon the path of the infinite, and He bends you with His might that His arrows may go swift and far. Let your bending in the Archer's hand be for gladness; for even as He loves the arrow that flies, so He loves also the bow that is stable."

Honoring and Blessing Parents

[Susanna] Nancy and David, if we would let in the full power of the love and devotion that it takes to be a parent, well, it would make our knees bend. Parenthood will bring you your greatest joys and your greatest worries. It is the most rewarding yet most challenging job on earth. Make no mistake about it, it is a sacred vocation. We as your community want to commend you on doing such a great job. On behalf of your family, friends, and the world at large, I thank you for bringing us the light that is Benjamin Simon.

[Susanna, with hands on heads and hearts] Nancy and David, may God's infinite love, strength, and wisdom be with you in this role. Benjamin is blessed to have you as his parents.

Candle Lighting

[Susanna] Nancy and David, following Greek and Jewish tradition, I ask each of you to light your candles from the large existing candle representing God's sublime illumination.

Now please take your lighted candles and jointly light a candle symbolic of Benjamin's life and soul.

I asked you both what you hoped to teach your child. Would you please read what you wrote to your son?

[David] Benjamin, we hope to teach you to learn as much as you can, to be yourself, to live life to the fullest, and to be happy.

The Naming

[Susanna] To honor Benjamin's Greek and Jewish heritage and both of his grandfathers, Benjamin will be given the Greek and Hebrew names of his grandfathers.

[Nancy] Demetrios is in honor of my father. It is derived from the name of the goddess Demeter, meaning "love the earth."

[Susanna] May Benjamin learn to love this earth and all of humanity who dwell upon it.

[David] Yisreal means "God's prince" and Lieb means "loved one." This is in honor of my father, who has passed on.

[Susanna] Benjamin is indeed God's unique manifestation upon this earth, loved and cherished beyond measure. We acknowledge that Grandpa [last name] is with us today spiritually. He remains in our hearts. He is missed.

The Blessing over the Wine

[Susanna] In both Jewish and Greek culture, the drinking of wine is a custom at important events. This cup of wine is symbolic of the cup of life. It is a blessed cup and the same chalice used at David and Nancy's wedding.

[David] At our wedding we drank together to celebrate our union. We drink again, for we have shared the greatest joy, that of participating in the creation of life.

[Susanna] Stin iyia sas! L'khayim! To your health! To life!

Honoring Grandparents

[Susanna] Beloved grandparents, this all began with you. Your fruit has multiplied. Your grandchild will benefit from your wisdom. He will bask in the warmth of your unconditional love, the kind only a grandparent can give—the spoiling kind. Grandparents hold a very special place in a child's heart.

Now Benjamin's paternal grandmother will read a poem she wrote especially for her grandson:

[Grandma Fran] Benjamin, you're a lucky fella,
With love from Fran and Jim and Stella,
And so much more from Mom and Dad,
You surely are a special lad.
We could not wait until you were born,
Oh yes, that was a happy morn.
You're as delicious as a bowl of candy,
And you're our Yankee Doodle Dandy.
Benjamin's maternal grandparents, Grandma and Grandpa [last name],
next read in alternating passages the lovely blessing that begins, "May you always
have enough happiness to keep you sweet, Enough trials to keep you strong ..."
[Susanna] We thank you. We honor you. God bless you. Now each of you kiss your grandson's little head!

Appointing and Honoring Godparent and the Godparent's Gift

Young Benjamin had one godparent, Nancy's sister, Cindy, a doctor. After my words to the godmother, requiring her to be a friend to her godchild, to share herself with him, to let him know that he is never alone, Cindy presented her gift. This was a toy doctor's bag, filled with health-related items. She explained that she and her sister used to play with a similar one when they were kids. The gift for Benjamin came with a wish that he have a lifelong pursuit of knowledge, and that he always prioritize love, happiness, and health.

[Susanna] Cindy, may God's love, compassion, and wisdom be with you in this role of godmother. I anoint you.

Baptism or Immersion in the Waters of Life

[Susanna] Water is the purest, clearest of liquids. In virtue of this, its natural character, it is the image of the spotless nature of divine spirit. Water has a significance in itself, as water. It is on account of its natural quality that it is consecrated and selected as the vehicle of a divine spirit.

We now use the gift of water to welcome this child into the world.

As Nancy held her son, I gently bathed his face, hands, and head.

Rose Petals and a Final Blessing

[Susanna] Rose petals represent life's sweet blessings—love, beauty, and poetry. We invite Benjamin's parents to gather a few rose petals and then gently sprinkle them upon the baby along with their personal blessings and good wishes for him for the many years to come.

Young one, listen to what I am about to say. Above you are the stars, below you is the earth, as time does pass, remember: Like the earth should your life be fertile, grounded in compassion. Like a star should your faith be constant, imbued with light. Let the powers of the mind and of the intellect guide you. Let your faith in life and love keep you strong. Let the power of the strength of your dedication make you happy, productive, and whole.

I would like to take a moment to thank the family for the delightful privilege of walking by their sides yet again. Some of the threads of the tapestries of our lives have been joined together. You are a gift for which I am profoundly grateful. To Benjamin, I say: Mazel tov! Na sou zisi! Congratulations! May you live a long life!

After my final words, our family of honor walked down the center aisle of the chapel to the accompaniment of our wonderful pianist playing, among other melodies, "Yankee Doodle Dandy," "New York, New York," and "Here Comes the Sun." A truly joyous recessional, after which all family and guests gathered for a group photo on the famous Low Library steps.

The Baby Naming Ceremony for Xavier Hasan

Baby Xavier's mother, Samantha, was of Irish Catholic heritage; his father, Hasan, a Palestinian Muslim. In the naming ceremony, to be held at home, these young parents wanted most of all to convey the importance of unity and a strong family, "the most precious gift," they wrote. Through a careful melding of Christian and Islamic elements, all were gathered and honored.

The ceremony:

Welcoming Remarks

After my opening remarks inviting all present to consider the miracle of a child, the miracle of this child, young Xavier, I shared these words from his parents:

[Susanna] When I asked our parents if they believed in God, they answered: "Yes, God is included and acknowledged every minute we live. God is the reason for all of our blessings and all our love and we recognize this every moment." About their child, they wrote: "He is an angel sent to us by God. We can stare at him for hours and actually feel the angel he is."

Having a child is monumental! There is nothing more life transforming. For these parents, the world has changed. The planets have realigned and the universe has expanded.

Now, some of you may have never experienced a ceremony like this before. This is an interfaith baby blessing celebration. Hasan and Samantha have thoughtfully and lovingly chosen every ritual, prayer, blessing, and reading you will hear and witness today in hopes of creating a ceremony that will reflect who they are and what they believe as a family. They rejoice in their commonalities and in their differences. God created diversity! If God had wanted only one flower in his garden, that is what God would have created. When I asked Hasan and Samantha how they hoped to raise their son, here is how they replied:

"He will learn both Catholicism and Islam, and spirituality, and the beauty of all religion. He will learn the basis of religion is to be thankful for what God gave us and to acknowledge a higher power and to thank God every day for being here."

So grandparents, be at peace. You have raised your children well. They are godly children with their hearts and minds in the right place. There is no need to fear. Courage is one of my favorite words. It comes from the Latin root word "cor," which means heart— literally, to be with heart. So courage is not having no fear; it is facing our fears with all of our heart, with love. Let us affirm that today, revel in that. Today, let us walk in light, God's eternal, transcendent, transformative light, brilliant and glorious beyond words.

Forming a Circle and Candle Lighting

[Susanna] We now ask that immediate family members and godparents form a circle around our family of honor. *When the circle was in place, I gave each individual a candle to hold.*

[Parents] We are humbled by the awesome responsibility of this moment.

We are filled with joy and trembling as we contemplate the tasks that lie before us: modeling love; teaching courage; instilling honesty, integrity, and responsibility.

May we come to embody the virtues we teach,

and may our child see in us the values and behaviors we hope to see in him.

[Susanna] We acknowledge this child as God created and God filled. We dedicate him to God. *As I said these words, I lighted a candle.*

[Parents] We thank God for you, our precious child.

[Susanna] I give you, friends and family, our parents' words: "A strong, unified family is the most precious gift. We each have a bright light, something unique and special to offer, and when we come together as one—as family— the light is even stronger."

Hasan, would you please take this lighted candle and go around lighting each person's candle within this circle—as your son's light, the light of his soul, a light that comes from God, will touch their light. First, Hasan will read this dedication.

[Hasan] We light these candles as a symbol of the collective sparks of life and love that is our family. As the flames join with one another, making one brighter and more lasting flame, so, too, do we come together. Much like the flame of this candle, when we share our love with each other our love is not diminished, but enhanced, and within us, the sparks of divinity burn even brighter.

After all the candles had been lit:

[Samantha] Our family is a circle of strength and love.

With every birth and every union the circle grows.

Every joy shared adds more love.

Every crisis faced together makes the circle grow stronger.

[Susanna] Family, look around you! Godparents and friends, look around you! You are the people who will help shape Xavier's life. A garden becomes more beautiful with each flower. It is the same with the garden of humanity. We become more beautiful with each culture, religion, and race. We are meant to enhance one another, to learn from one another. Nothing is diminished in God's eyes. We are here to learn to see with the eyes of the heart.

Xavier will understand this firsthand because of his combined heritage. Where others may struggle to learn the meaning of respect, tolerance, and understanding, Xavier will live it. In the world he inherits, this is crucial. He will be, by virtue of who he is, a teacher, a peacemaker. How blessed!

In Christianity it is said that God is love. In the Koran, God is given ninety-nine names. One of God's most powerful names in the Koran is "the Most Merciful." I put it to you that there is no mercy without love and no love without mercy.

We need one another.

Will you please extinguish your candles and everyone kindly be seated— after we share hugs.

Salaam aleikum. Peace be with you.

A Blessing and Anointing

[Susanna] We will now bestow upon Xavier his first formal blessing and I will anoint his head with oil.

Blessed be this child of God, Xavier Hasan [last name], whose very beginning is as our own and in whom we see infinite potential.

Blessed be this child of love, who reflects the love of God. May he feel a spirit of kinship with all creation.

Blessed be this child of wisdom, whose ever-expanding mind will touch the font of knowing. May he learn to listen to the words and feelings of others, and to the voice of God in prayer, so that he will gain understanding.

Blessed be this child of eternity. May his path lead him to the highest pinnacles of life, love, joy, and wisdom. May his life be long and good upon this earth.

The Parents' Promises

The parents responded to each question in turn.

[Susanna] In Christian tradition, parents make spiritual promises to their child. We have adapted those promises to reflect what is in these parents' hearts.

Samantha and Hasan, do you promise to love Xavier as God has loved you?

Will you teach him of the love of God, for God is love and love comes from God?

Do you promise to see and honor Xavier as soul, as that which is uniquely him?

Do you promise to guide Xavier and give him freedom to live the life that is his calling?

Parents, I asked you each what you hope, pray, wish, or dream for your child, and how you saw your role as parents. Please read your words to your son.

[Hasan] Xavier, we hope and pray that you see God in everything, every breath, and that you will be happy and safe. We hope we can put you in a position to accomplish your goals in life.

[Samantha] Xavier, our role is to allow you room to grow, and not smother you. It is our responsibility to let you make mistakes and help you learn from your mistakes, to help you believe in yourself. We hope to teach you to be confident, nice, kind, humble, and to treat others the way you would like to be treated. We hope to teach you to appreciate what you have, and to give you good values and morals.

[Susanna] Our parents told me that they hope their son will inherit from his mother her kind heart, to always see the good in people. They hope that he will inherit from his father his kind and humble heart as well, but also the ability to be cocky and tough and stern—if and when need be!

Hasan and Samantha, Gandhi once said, "Your life is your greatest example and teaching to your children." Live your words, and your son will learn them.

I ended this portion of the ceremony by bestowing a blessing upon the parents' heads.

A Blessing and Prayer

[Susanna] Xavier, may you always feel loved and cherished in your parents' home.

May you know that each sunrise is a promise of a new beginning.

May no storm last so long as to shadow your spirit.

May you hear God's voice in the wind and in the sound of your own laughter.

May you see God's face in every person you meet, in every flower, and in every living thing.

May you know that you are never alone, that you are guided by an eternal force, loving and powerful beyond measure.

May your days be good and long upon this earth. Amen.

[Susanna] The "Our Father" is one of the most significant prayers of the Christian tradition. It calls upon God in great trust and confidence. Let us join together as we pray:

Our Father, who art in heaven, hallowed be thy name.

Thy kingdom come, thy will be done, on earth as it is in heaven.

Give us this day our daily bread, and forgive us our trespasses

As we forgive those who have trespassed against us.

And lead us not into temptation, but deliver us from evil. Amen.

Universal Baptism

Xavier's Muslim grandparents had brought water from the River Jordan in Palestine to be used for the baby's baptism, a wonderful acknowledgment of the appropriateness of a universal baptism within a Christian-Muslim ceremony.

[Susanna] At the very dawn of creation, Almighty God used his spirit to breathe life into the waters, making them the wellspring of life. We therefore use the blessing of water to welcome this child into this world. In doing so, we dedicate him to God. May God's illumination reside with you, now and forever. God's peace be upon you, Xavier.

After I poured the water gently upon the baby's head, Grandma Linda, Samantha's mother, came up and also poured some upon his head.

[Susanna] We now invite Grandpa Mohammad [last name] to recite the first *sura* of the Koran, considered the door and mystical essence of the Koran. As is traditional in Islam, he will quietly speak the sura in Arabic into his grandson's ear.

And here is an English translation:

"In the name of the merciful and compassionate God.

Praise belongs to God, the Lord of the worlds,

he the merciful, the compassionate,

he the ruler of the day of judgment.

Thee we serve and thee we ask for aid.

Guide us in the right path,

the path of those thou art gracious to,

not of those thou art wroth with, nor of those who err."

Salaam Aleikum, Xavier Hasan [last name]. May you live these mystical words of peace. I anoint your head with oil.

Honoring Grandparents and Those Who Have Gone Before

Among those we remembered was Hasan's sister Nadia, who had died of SIDS at three months of age. She and the other departed family members were acknowledged as Xavier's angels, watching over him as he grows. To everyone's delight, baby Xavier's great-grandfather Saverio was with us on this day, and to him I offered the following words:

[Susanna] There is an old blessing that says, "May you live to see your children's children." I can only imagine how blessed it must be to see your children's grandchildren! We honor you.

It is in honor of all family members past and present that we offer this quote by Alice Walker: "To acknowledge our ancestors means we are aware that we did not make ourselves, that the line stretches all the way back, perhaps to God. The grace with which we embrace life, in spite of the pain, the sorrows, is always a measure of what has gone before."

Will the grandparents now please come forward? Your kids tell me that you are indeed *amazing* grandparents.

In the questionnaire, Hasan and Samantha had written with such heartfelt love and appreciation about their parents. Here are just a few of the comments I shared at the ceremony:

[Susanna, to Hasan's parents] Your son told me that he would like to emulate for his own son how you treated him and his brother. Quite a tribute! He told me that as early as the age of five, you taught him about budgets. You always gave him a say in important family decisions. You taught him to think independently and analytically and he always had an opportunity to lobby his case. So you gave him his beginnings as a lawyer—with a sense of fairness.

[To Samantha's parents] Samantha told me she would emulate for her son how her father would go to the ends of the earth for her. She remembers all his special touches, such as fresh roses from the garden left in her car as a surprise. Growing up, she loved having lunch made by her mother with special notes tucked inside. She says that above all she wants to emulate the way her mom made her feel, that special bond that no one else but a mother can give.

On a day like today, we see a sublime torch, a lineage of love passed from generation to generation. Plato's words: love is immortality.

Grandparents, on your grandson's blessing day, we honor you. We thank you.

The Blessing from the Grandparents

[Susanna] Now I am going to call each grandparent forward by name one at a time. When your name is called, please step forward and gently place your hand on the baby's head to offer him a blessing. Please repeat after me and then continue in your own words: "God bless you, Xavier, I pray that ..." Speak from your heart. And be at peace, this is not a performance!

Appointing Godparents and the Godparents' Spiritual Gifts

After calling the godparents forward, my opening words were to remind the gathering that children need many sources of support, from the community at large and from those chosen as spiritual mentors or godparents. Children need other guides, for sometimes parents are just too close.

[Susanna] Cesar and Jennifer, you have been chosen by Hasan and Samantha as spiritual mentors for their child. They think most highly of you, trusting you with the spiritual care of their son. You each have unique strengths, offerings they hope you will share with Xavier. After all, there is no greater gift we can give than our own spirits.

Samantha and Hasan had written in the questionnaire and had told me during our conversations how highly they valued their chosen mentors, and I shared some of their words with our guests. Jennifer, they said, was kind, caring, smart, confident, modest, reliable, and loyal. Cesar, a friend of Hasan's since high school and like a brother to him, was a solid example of a hard worker and a generous person "who would give you the shirt off his back." Baby Xavier would be in good hands.

[Parents] Cesar and Jennifer, will you support us in the spiritual mentoring of our child? Will you be there to listen to him, and to help and advise him, if necessary?

[Godparents] We will.

Their spiritual gifts to their new godson were words to live by: from Cesar, a born-again Christian, a quotation from the Bible, framed with a beautiful picture; from Jennifer, a plaque with a reading about the importance of learning and the life of the mind.

[Susanna] Godparents, inspire Xavier, be a friend to him, share yourselves with him. Allow him to dream great dreams. Nourish his soul. Help him discover his own majesty. Show him the wonders of the world.

God bless you, Jennifer and Cesar, godmother and godfather of Xavier, may you be granted the love, compassion, and wisdom needed in your role. I now anoint you.

A Closing Blessing for All

[Susanna] Before we end the ceremony, I would like to thank the family for the privilege of walking by their side today. You are the gift. I am humbly grateful for this gift. Islam means peace. We dedicate this ceremony to peace.

May God bless and keep you. May God's countenance shine upon you and be gracious unto you. May God's presence be with you and grant you peace. Amen. Ma'salaama.

Rose Petals and a Final Blessing

[Susanna] This child has been blessed, welcomed, and dedicated to God. His godparents have been appointed.

Xavier Hasan, may you be blessed beneath the wings of angels. Be blessed with love, be blessed with peace.

I sprinkle rose petals upon our honored child. And we now invite each of you to come up one by one. Please gather a few rose petals and gently sprinkle them upon the baby, along with your own personal blessings and good wishes for Xavier for the many years to come.

Congratulations!

PART IV

Down the Years

RAISING YOUR CHILD IN SPIRITUAL WISDOM

The baby naming ceremony is just the beginning, after all, the formal "launching" of a much-loved son or daughter. For many interfaith or intercultural couples, further questions and further decisions will sooner or later be addressed. The following comments are typical of many I have received from new parents:

"My husband is Jewish and I'm Catholic. Most of the information that I've found about raising interfaith children pertains to 'picking' one faith over the other. Since my husband doesn't really practice his religion but feels that he wants our child to 'be Jewish,' I am totally conflicted about the right way to proceed."

"We aren't committed to practicing a specific faith. But we don't want our child to lack an identity around religion in some way and are not sure what to do."

The first observation I make to these couples, and that I make to you now, is that there is no one "right way" to raise a child in an interfaith or nontraditional home and atmosphere. Parents are choosing various routes: one religion, its practices and observances, will be emphasized; both religions will be celebrated; spiritual awareness not rooted in any particular religion will be encouraged. A family may elect to emphasize the cultural aspects of their traditions, but not the religious. Another family may decide to embark on an entirely new path—Quakerism, perhaps, Buddhism, Sufism, or Baha'i—a path that, after exploration and thought, feels most at home to all family members.

Here, then, are some ideas and suggestions on how to sustain the inclusive, welcoming, tolerant, and joyous nature of the naming day through the life of your growing child.

Calming Grandparents' Fears

We have come a long way in the past decade or so on how we view mixed marriages and the children of mixed marriages. Most young people living in modern communities see any biases and prejudices as a lingering generational issue of the past. But many individuals in the older generation do still have a hard time making peace with the interfaith couple.

I have worked with families in which one side has "disowned" their child for marrying out of the faith or race. This is excruciating for the disowned child, now an adult, and in fact it's something that he or she never quite gets over. Deep inside, we all long to be loved unconditionally by our parents.

To grandparents who contemplate severing connection with their children,

I tell a story related to me by my aunt. Her neighbor, a Jewish man who lived next door for decades, had disowned his daughter because she married a Christian. In old age, diagnosed with cancer, he was nearing the end of his life. When his daughter was informed of this, she decided to take his three granddaughters, whom he had never met, to his bedside. Friends advised her not to, as they thought it probably would leave her even more scarred, but she was determined.

We don't know exactly what went on at that visit, but later, the neighbor said this to my aunt: "Lena, what have I done? I have deprived myself of the love of my daughter and my three grandchildren for all these years. And for what? For what?"

It's a powerful story.

Many grandparents have asked for my advice. They tell me of their feelings of hurt, disappointment, or even betrayal. Sometimes they are very angry. I remind them of a truth perhaps best expressed in the words of Kahlil Gibran's "On Children," so often requested as a naming ceremony reading: "Your children are not your children. They are the sons and daughters of Life's longing for itself." Parents must set their children free.

And I often tell this story to the grandparents who say they feel their children have made a terrible, terrible mistake by marrying outside the faith. A father went to a rabbi and asked, "Rebbe, my son is lost. He is going down the wrong path, and try as I might, I simply cannot reach him. What shall I do?" The rabbi was quick with his response: "Love him more than ever." True love, after all, is unconditional.

Even if Grandmother or Grandfather, perhaps with some reluctance, accepted the marriage of a son or daughter outside the family faith, when a grandchild appears, old tensions can reemerge, as we've seen in some of the personal histories related earlier. The anger, the unhappiness, the fear often first surfaces around the planning for a naming ceremony. And when two sets of grandparents are part of the picture—four or perhaps more individuals, if the older generation includes divorce and remarriage—the emotional currents and conversations are complicated and stressful.

An expectant father, awaiting the birth of his first child, said that he and his wife had talked over with their own parents their intention to raise the child interfaith and their interest in interfaith education programs for young children. A spiritual, nonreligious baby naming ceremony would be the "kickoff" to these carefully thought-out plans. His parents and his wife's dad, this young father-to-be wrote, were completely supportive of their decisions. "Unfortunately," he added, "as we anticipated, [my wife's] mom and stepdad were very disappointed. They are having a difficult time digesting the idea of the child not being raised Catholic, not having a 'real' christening, etc. They expressed concern about the child being confused and having no religion, but more significantly, cannot stomach the idea of the child not being Catholic. Right now, they are holding out hope that we will change our minds."

He asked if I had any suggestions "to help bring them around."

We talked over the ideas about approaching grandparents with loving respect but as a united front—that is, as partners who will be making the decisions about how to welcome and raise the new offspring. We talked about the need to set boundaries with the older generation, again firmly, with loving respect. And we talked about the need, when confronting disapproving or disappointed grandparents, to speak in the "we"— "we have decided to … we really have given this a lot of thought … we plan to … we feel that …" I often notice that a spouse will suggest it was his wife's or her husband's idea to raise the child one way or another, out of fear of grandparents' disapproval. But the attempt to avoid confrontation in the moment can only lead to layers of misunderstandings and unspoken feelings later on, often laced with layers of anger and resentment. Let it be known in no uncertain terms that your decisions about raising children reflect both you and your partner, and what you believe are for the good of your marriage and new family.

The unfortunate truth, however, is that there's a limit to what can be done to "bring them around."

Sometimes, no matter the amount of outreach and communication on the part of the parents, grandparents remain intractable. If you know you have done everything in your power to respect and include them, conveyed your feelings with honesty and compassion to help them understand your path and the choices you will make for your children—let go. Give your parents space. They need to accept and, ideally, come to peace with your decisions in their own time. We cannot control others' feelings and behaviors, only how we respond to them.

On "Picking" One Religion

Many parents believe that bringing up the children in one religion is the simplest, cleanest, and perhaps safest way to go. And sometimes choosing one faith really works well.

Jacob is the son of a Holocaust survivor; Maria is Italian Catholic. Though her faith is strong, Maria understood Jacob's family history and how much Judaism meant to him. After much thought and discussion on both their parts, it was decided that the children were to be raised Jewish, while Maria would keep her Catholic faith and the children would be taught to respect their mother's beliefs.

Maria does sometimes have "twinges," she said, when she wishes that her children would be with her at Sunday mass. For the most part, however, all are pleased with their decision. Her own Catholic parents are glad that the children are being raised with some religious orientation rather than none.

Is it necessary for all family members to move in lockstep along the same religious (or nonreligious) paths? I don't think so. With mutual understanding and respect, there is room to accept and accommodate individual needs and histories. One woman, a mother of three youngsters, grew up in a traditionally Catholic household, was baptized as an infant, received communion at seven, and was confirmed at age twelve. "As I matured," she says, "I began questioning many of the tenets of the Church, particularly dogma and rules, and I left." Her husband grew up as a Christian Science practitioner. The family now— "off and on, not every week"—goes to services at a Unitarian church, where the children have been enjoying the religious education programs they've been attending since preschool.

Of herself today, she says: "I still love the resplendence of Catholic churches. I adore the music. So on occasion I will go to High Mass on holidays, to be inspired. I will sit in an empty church for peace. When times are tough or a loved one has died, I will go to a church and light a candle and pray. There remains in me some of that little Catholic school girl." And that's all right.

But the parent whose religion the children will not follow should seriously consider the implications; it's not a decision to be made lightly. Honestly identify and evaluate your feelings and thoughts. It can be a soul-searching process. You might, for example, easily accept the seasonal or cultural traditions: the children will observe Jewish holidays and will visit the Catholic grandparents on Easter and Christmas and receive Christmas presents. One parent had no problem with "the trappings," as she called them. But the child growing up within a particular tradition will probably be encouraged or required to participate in periods of religious instruction.

If your child will be preparing for his or her bar or bat mitzvah, what will be involved? Will you be comfortable supporting him or her, perhaps devoting some of your time, in the study of the Torah? If your child will be preparing for confirmation, what lessons will he or she be learning? Can you be comfortable with those lessons? One mother in an interfaith marriage had attended Lutheran school throughout her childhood, and had come to consider the old Sunday school and Saturday Bible classes "brainwashing." She now struggled with the idea of her young daughter being raised in her husband's Catholic faith.

These are among the issues to consider carefully as you reach the important decision of "picking" one religion for your child.

"Mom, What Are We?"

Once children enter school or start spending time at playmates' homes, they begin to become aware of a variety of issues related to religious identification, and they can begin to have questions. These may not necessarily be questions about religious or spiritual beliefs as such. Youngsters are often charmed by or perhaps somewhat envious of something a friend is "into" while they are not.

Four-year-old Jack was invited to a seder at his best friend Lucas's house during Passover. Lucas was the youngest child in the family and had been designated to ask the four questions, beginning "Why is this night different from all other nights of the year?" He performed admirably and all the grownups congratulated him. Jack was both excited for his friend and feeling a little left out. Back home, he told his mom that he could have said the questions too, and why didn't they have a dinner like that? Jack's mom explained that since their family was not Jewish, they did not celebrate Passover. Jack said, "Well, what are we?"

Five-year-old Caroline had shared many playdates and park outings since toddlerhood with Annmarie, a neighbor in their apartment building. When the two girls started school, Caroline entered the local public school; Annmarie went to a private Catholic girl's school, and headed out every morning in the uniform of white blouse, pale gray jumper, and red-and-white plaid pinafore. Caroline fell in love with this outfit and wanted to know why she couldn't wear one too. "You have to be a student in the Catholic school to wear that," her mother said. Caroline begged to go to Annmarie's school.

Then at some point along the way, as he grows and learns and experiences more of life, your child may reach his own answer to the question "What are we?" or more particularly, "What am I, what do I believe?" The mother of a young teenager told this story:

"I was raised Catholic, my husband was Protestant. Neither of us was religiously active, and when our son, James, was born, we decided to baptize him in the waters of the Caribbean in a nondenominational, nondogmatic baby blessing that was a sacred welcoming. It was private, personal, and meaningful, in God's cathedral.

"But how to raise him? We ended up sending our son to an Episcopal school, primarily for the quality of the academic education, but also for the spiritual component. The rituals felt very close to Catholicism without the rigidity, yet it was Protestant for my husband. Church attendance on Sundays was not mandatory. But this is what impressed us most: the school taught a different religion each year. The children learned about Christianity, Judaism, Islam, Buddhism, Hinduism, Taoism, and Native American spirituality.

"James is by nature a thinker. He has wrestled with the concept of God and the meaning of life for years. One day, when he was eleven, he announced to us that he thought himself to be Buddhist. He told us that he did not identify with Judeo-Christian beliefs, or the language used in the Bible or at church. He related to the Buddhist tenet of 'doing no harm' and the Buddha's desire to help humanity. He was drawn to its sense of the sacred without having to identify with a deity. He liked 'the way they talk,' he said.

"We supported this. We bought him books, including *Wide Awake: A Buddhist Guide for Teens* by Diana Winston and *Zen Flesh, Zen Bones* compiled by Paul Reps and Nyogen SenZaki. They spoke to him. Now a teenager, he says he hopes to become a professor of philosophy. To me, what's important is that he finds something that connects him back to himself and the world, something that will nourish him through the difficulties of life."

So to answer the question: "Mom, what are we?"

If you plan to raise your child celebrating both his mother's and his father's religious traditions, it is best to answer honestly and, with a young child, simply. For example: "We are an interfaith family. Mommy was raised Christian, Daddy was raised Jewish [Muslim, Hindu, Sikh]. We value both of our traditions so we celebrate Christmas and Hanukah [Christmas and Eid, Christmas and Divali]. We pray to the same God in different ways. There are many different religions in the world. They are different ways of praying to God."

If you are atheist or agnostic, or perhaps still uncertain about your own beliefs when your child begins to pose questions in this regard, be honest about that as well. Together, hand in hand, you may begin a spiritual exploration—by reading, by attending services. Indeed, your children may teach you. From this open approach, children learn valuable lessons: It's okay not to know everything. It's okay to ask questions.

Perhaps most important: Your children will feel supported by you. They will learn that they are not alone in their search. They will learn that it's normal, even necessary, to openly explore the most profound issues in life.

As your child gets older, matures, and has greater exposure to the world of people and ideas, your conversations can become more detailed. Your children may surprise you! They will have their own ideas.

Not "Instead Of," but "In Addition To"

More interfaith couples than ever before are electing to raise their children with the knowledge of both parents' religious traditions. In these households, two sets of holidays—and sometimes three—are celebrated. These parents feel their children are enriched by two faiths and cultures, twice blessed.

At the same time, many parents in interfaith homes have asked me, "Will our children grow up confused?" This is a concern fostered by some religious institutions, which warn about the confusion children can experience from celebrating two traditions. But these reports are usually based on surveys taken from their congregations, and thus may be considered biased. If this is your worry, you should know that no "proof" exists of any damage done to children from living in interfaith households, no indication that these youngsters are any more uncertain or torn or spiritually lacking than are children raised in single-faith households.

My own experience in working with the adult children of interfaith, intercultural marriages, in fact, leads to another conclusion. These individuals almost always embody something quite wonderful—a broad, tolerant view of the world, accepting of diversity. In my opinion, they are peacemakers and teachers, simply by virtue of who they are; where others may struggle with concepts of respect, tolerance, and understanding, they have lived it. To me, they represent a hope toward a promised land, embodied in the words of Emerson: "Unity in diversity." No us versus them. No me versus you. Just one human family living side by side on this small but precious earth.

I look at a garden and think, with each unique flower the garden becomes more beautiful. Hybrids are beautiful, too, sometimes even more beautiful. So it is with every faith, culture, and ethnicity, the garden of humanity becomes ever more magnificent.

Do remember always that the respect you and your partner demonstrate toward each other's beliefs and traditions will be communicated to your children. Respect, honesty, and clear communication are key, for children sense when there's something amiss with parents. They sense hidden agendas. In Gandhi's words: "Your life is a message to your children." In Aesop's words: "Example is the best precept." The greatest lessons we convey to our children are not through our words, but through who we are.

Christmas Trees, Menorahs ... and Teaching Moments

A mother spoke about raising her soon-to-be born second child as she and her husband had done with their first. "We want our kids to understand that his parents are of both religions, and we want them to understand what is involved in each. We're very happy with the results so far. Last year our son, Benjamin, was asked at school, 'What do you have at home, a menorah or a Christmas tree?' and he replied, 'Both!' We were so proud. The teacher asked me about this later, and I explained that Ben is growing up in a Jewish/ Catholic household. We plan the same for this new baby."

I love to hear about parents—and children—celebrating diversity, not proselytizing, but simply explaining, this is who we are, this is what we think, this is how our kids are learning about religion and spirituality. Keep an open mind and heart, and you will probably also come across many opportunities to help your child understand about differences among people, and about the importance of religious symbols to so many.

Here's an example: In the lobby of one family's apartment building, decorations had been put up around the holidays—a small tree with white lights, fragrant green wreaths with red bows, and some clever figures made from twisted gold wire depicting reindeer and snowmen. Leaving for school one morning, Anna and her eight-year-old son Peter saw that the display had been removed; the lobby was its usual unadorned self. Over the next few days it came to light that several tenants had objected loudly to the decorations and insisted that if they remained, a menorah should be included. Subsequently, each household received a form from the management, a checklist of four or five options for next year's holiday season—a tree and a menorah, potted seasonal plants, no decorations at all, and so on. A vote would be tallied and everyone would be notified about the final decision.

Peter, a bright and inquisitive youngster, thought all this was kind of silly. It was just some nice stuff, he said, why couldn't everybody enjoy them? This was an opportunity, which his parents acted on, to talk a little about the need to accommodate several points of view and feelings in public spaces that everyone shares. It wasn't just a matter of "keeping everyone happy," Peter's father said, it went a little deeper than that. Their family might consider the tree and wreaths as pretty decorations, but others saw the tree as a Christian custom and therefore a religious symbol, which offended them if their own religious symbols were not included as well. It was important to respect the sensitivities of all sides, and probably a democratic vote was the best way to accomplish that.

Another youngster and her parents lived in a neighborhood that included several Muslim families. At the local pharmacy chain store, one of the salespersons at the checkout counter was a young woman who wore a hijab, the traditional head scarf. Seven-year-old Isabella asked her mother about this, why the salesperson had on a hat inside. Mother and daughter did some Internet research and read about the hijab and its meaning in Muslim culture. One day Isabella saw two older women walking by on the street dressed in flowing black garments that covered all parts of their bodies, including their faces except for small, horizontal openings across their eyes. Isabella was fascinated.

She had a lot of questions. That clothing looked hot, was it comfortable? Did they like wearing it? Was it hard to see where they were going? Did those ladies mind that some people on the street were staring at them? She and her mother did some further research about Muslim customs, and Isabella got information that helped to answer her questions. This parent said: "I remember when I was a kid, nuns used to wear the long habits with the starched white headdresses, and I was always so curious about that. I asked my grandmother once if they had to cut off their hair, if they wore those clothes all the time, and she said something like, 'I have no idea, that's just what they do.' It wasn't much of an answer. I try to answer my kids' questions, so they learn about other people and other ways of life."

It's part of raising a child in spiritual wisdom. It's part of learning about the world and its citizens.

The Search for a New Spiritual Home

A Mormon/Catholic couple asked for suggestions about a spiritual community for themselves and their growing family. Their prior religious affiliations had faded over the years and both parents had officially left their respective churches. But where should they turn? It's a question I often hear from interfaith as well as unaffiliated or nondenominational parents, and my advice to them was as follows:

Contact the organizations (some are listed in my resource directory) that draw you. Ask them to send you literature. Ask them to supply you with a list of the communities closest to your home. Then, attend services. Meet some of the congregants and spiritual leaders. Sit in on the classes that are organized for children. In the case of the Mormon/Catholic couple, I told them to church shop! As I mentioned earlier in this book, you will know when you have found your spiritual home. You will feel it.

That process of church shopping and exploration may, in fact, lead you to a deeper awareness of the spiritual nature of life than anything you previously experienced. You may question more, read more, think more. The mother of now-eight-year-old twins had this to say: "We, together as a family, are spending some time looking for a spiritual community. Interestingly, I found myself drawn to elements of Judaism, there's a lot of humanity there, though neither my husband nor I are Jewish.

"I grew up in a fairly typical Methodist family, and I followed what the church said until around college time I just drifted away. What I realize is that when you're born into a religion, there's a lot you do out of habit, routine, a lot you just kind of take for granted and go through the motions. This quest we're on now—still underway!—seems more thoughtful and ultimately meaningful." Her daughters are very much involved in the quest. "They're young, of course," this mom said, "but they've had some interesting reactions. They're thinking about what all this means, and that's good."

The members of another family, also exploring various organizations, were strongly attracted to the practices and ideals of the Religious Society of Friends, the Quakers. They attended silent meetings in a Quaker house in their city. Said this parent: "Our nine-year-old after one meeting said she really wanted 'something fancier,' as she put it. We had recently gone to the funeral mass for a close family friend, an older woman and Catholic. Katy was very taken with things going on in the service. She loved the incense and the chanting. This appealed to her."

This family might do well to investigate Buddhism, Hinduism, or perhaps a more ecumenical sect of Christianity. One can still have meaningful and moving rituals that feel spiritual, without a theistic view. As human beings, we have a need to celebrate major rites of passage, to take part in rituals. If you are atheist or agnostic parents, your child may one day want to learn more about God and religion, may even gravitate to "something fancier." Support her search, with love. Our children may have different needs than ours, and those should be respected.

Many families do choose a third way. I am thinking of Jared and Kate, Jewish and Christian respectively, who are raising their two children Buddhist. Ahmed and Julia, Muslim and Greek Orthodox, are raising their children in the Baha'i faith. For me, the essence of religion is to connect one back to the transcendent. If you are on your own "church shopping," consider the many options you have. And be courageous in this pursuit of what is right for your family.

In the course of serving and getting to know so many new parents, older parents, brand-new babies, and growing children over the years, it has seemed to me that the definition of family is evolving—to mean, on a personal level, the people who love, care, and support us through joy and hardship, through thick and thin. In an ideal world, we will further evolve to think in terms of the global human family—all citizens of this earth, beautifully diverse and rich, with respect for our differences, to be celebrated.

And so perhaps a fitting way to end *Bless This Child* is with the following quotations. As you will see, the golden rule appears in some form in all religions and beliefs.

- Baha'i: Blessed is he who preferreth his brother before himself. *(Bahá'u'lláh)*

- Buddhism: Hurt not others in ways that you yourself would find hurtful. *(Udana-Varga 5:18)*

- Christianity: Do unto others as you would have them do unto you. *(Bible, Luke 6:13)*

- Confucianism: Do not do to others what you do not want them to do to you. *(Analects 15:23)*
- Hinduism: This is the sum of duty: Do naught unto others that would cause you pain if done to you. *(Mahabharata 5:1517)*
- Islam: No one of you is a believer until you desire for another that which you desire for yourself. *(The Sunnah, from the Hadith)*
- Jainism: A man should wander about treating all creatures as he himself would be treated. *(Sutrakritanga 1.11.33)*
- Judaism: Love your neighbor as yourself. *(Leviticus 19:18)*
- Native American: Respect for all life is the foundation. *(The Great Law of Peace)*
- Sikhism: Don't create hatred with anyone, as God is within everyone. *(Guru Granth Sahib)*
- Sufism: You must see in the heart of another the temple of God. *(Hazrat Inayat Khan: The Art of Being)*
- Taoism: I am good to the man who is good to me; likewise; I am also good to the bad man. *(Tao Te Ching)*
- Zoroastrianism: Whatever is disagreeable to yourself do not do unto others. *(Shayast-na-shayast 13:29)*
- Wicca: And if it harm no one, do what thou wilt. *(The Wiccan Rede)*
- Secular: We should conduct ourselves toward others as we would have them act toward us. *(Aristotle, 385 B.C.)*

A Final Word

This was sent to me once as a mass e-mail, and I have since passed it on to many. I can think of no better conclusion to this book or better gift for a young mother or expectant friend. It also makes a lovely keepsake to put with your child's other special belongings. Moms, get out your hankies!

"The Gifts of Being a Mother," from *Everyday Miracles* by Dale Hanson Bourke:

A conversation between friends ...

We are sitting at lunch when my friend casually mentions that she and her husband are thinking of "starting a family." "We're taking a survey," she says, half-joking. "Do you think I should have a baby?"

"It will change your life," I say, carefully keeping my tone neutral.

"I know," she says, "no more sleeping in on weekends, no more spontaneous vacations."

But that is not what I meant at all.

I look at my friend, trying to decide what to tell her. I want her to know what she will never learn in childbirth classes. I want to tell her that the physical wounds of childbearing will heal, but that becoming a mother will leave her with an emotional wound so raw that she will forever be vulnerable. I consider warning her that she will never again read a newspaper without asking, "What if that had been my child?" That every plane crash, every house fire will haunt her. That when she sees pictures of starving children, she will wonder if anything could be worse than watching your child die.

I look at her carefully manicured nails and stylish suit and think that no matter how sophisticated she is, becoming a mother will reduce her to the primitive level of a bear protecting her cub. That an urgent call of "Mom!" will cause her to drop a soufflé or her best crystal without a moment's hesitation. I feel I should warn her that no matter how many years she has invested in her career, she will be professionally derailed by motherhood.

She might arrange for childcare, but one day she will be going into an important business meeting and she will think of her baby's sweet smell. She will have to use every ounce of her discipline to keep from running home, just to make sure her baby is all right.

I want my friend to know that everyday decisions will no longer be routine. That a five-year-old boy's desire to go to the men's room rather than the women's at McDonald's will become a major dilemma. That right there, in the midst of clattering trays and screaming children, issues of independence and gender identity will be weighed against the prospect that a child molester may be lurking in the restroom.

However decisive she may be at the office, she will second-guess herself constantly as a mother. Looking at my attractive friend, I want to assure her that eventually she will shed the pounds of pregnancy, but she will never feel the same about herself. That her life, now so important, will be of less value to her once she has a child. That she would give it up in a moment to save her offspring, but will also begin to hope for more years—not to accomplish her own dreams, but to watch her children accomplish theirs.

I want her to know that a cesarean scar or shiny stretch marks will become badges of honor. My friend's relationship with her husband will change, but not in the way she thinks. I wish she could understand how much more you can love a man who is careful to powder the baby or who never hesitates to play with his child. I think she should know that she will fall in love with him again for reasons she would now find very unromantic.

I wish my friend could sense the bond she will feel with women throughout history who have tried to stop war, prejudice, and drunk driving. I hope she will understand why I can think rationally about most issues, but become temporarily insane when I discuss the threat of nuclear war to my children's future. I want to describe to my friend the exhilaration of seeing your child learn to ride a bike. I want to capture for her the belly laugh of a baby who is touching the soft fur of a dog or a cat for the first time. I want her to taste the joy that is so real, it actually hurts.

My friend's quizzical look makes me realize that tears have formed in my eyes. "You'll never regret it," I finally say. Then I reach across the table, squeeze my friend's hand and offer a silent prayer for her, and for me, and for all of the mere mortal women who stumble their way into this most wonderful of callings. That of being a Mother.

I wish you much joy in your journey as a family.

A Resource Directory

<u>Certificates for Baby Blessing Ceremonies</u>

- Interfaith baby naming:
  A Good Company
  899 S. Plymouth Ct. #2206
  Chicago, IL 60605
  (312) 922-5888
  www.agoodcompany.com

- Birth and baptismal documents and certificates:
  Documents and Design
  32 Sewell St.
  Lake George, NY 12845
  (518) 668-4334
  www.documentsanddesigns.com

- Jewish baby naming:
  J. Levine Co.
  5 West 30th St.
  New York, NY 10001
  (212) 695-6888
  www.levinejudaica.com

- Baby naming certificates, birth announcements, and family trees:
  Elaine Adler
  (781) 861-9679
  www.elaineadler.com

- Jewish baby naming and baby blessing certificates:
  Artistic Judaic Promotions
  (877) 443-8836
  www.ajp.com

- Baptismal certificates:
  Christianbook.com
  140 Summit St.
  Peabody, MA 01960
  (800) 247-4784
  www.christianbook.com

- Victorian certificates:
  Grandma's Attic
  8755 Bluebird Road
  Rogers, AR 72756
  (479) 616-1466
  www.grandmas-attic.com

Congregations

Several spiritual communities welcome interfaith families. Unitarian Universalist Churches and the American Ethical Union serve as spiritual homes for many blended families. We have listed below the information for the headquarters of these congregations. You may contact them for general information and also to find a location nearest to your home.

- Unitarian-Universalist Association of Congregations
  25 Beacon St.
  Boston, MA 02108
  (617) 742-2100
  www.uua.org

- Quaker Information Center (at Friends Center)
  1501 Cherry St.
  Philadelphia, PA 19102
  (215) 241-7024
  www.quakerinfo.org

- American Ethical Union (of the New Society of Ethical Culture)
  2 West 64th St.
  New York, NY 10023
  (212) 873-6500
  www.aeu.org

- American Humanist Association
  1777 T St., NW
  Washington, D.C. 20009-7125
  (202) 238-9088
  www.americanhumanist.org

- Interfaith Community
  ("provides a neutral and affirming place for interfaith families to connect,"
  with programs and information for Jewish-Christian families)
  475 Riverside Drive, Suite 1945
  New York, NY 10115
  (212) 870-2544
  www.interfaithcommunity.org

- Rabbinic Center for Research and Counseling
  (offers a list of rabbis who will officiate at interfaith ceremonies and offers
  information on raising children in interfaith homes)
  128 East Dudley
  Westfield, NJ 07090
  (908) 233-0419
  www.rcronline.org

- Interfaith Families Project
  (for Jewish-Christian families)
  P.O. Box 5413
  Takoma Park, MD 20913
  (301) 270-6337
  www.iffp.net

- Interfaith Community Church
  1763 NW 62nd St.
  Seattle, WA 98107
  (206) 783-1618
  www.interfaithcommunitychurch.org

- InterFaithways
  (welcoming interfaith couples into the Jewish community)
  8339 Old York Road
  Suite 209
  Elkins Park, PA 19027
  (215) 207-0990
  www.interfaithways.org

- Sufi Order International
  P.O. Box 480
  New Lebanon, NY 12125
  (518) 794-7834
  www.sufiorder.org

- Buddhist Churches of America
  BCA Headquarters
  1710 Octavia St.
  San Francisco, CA 94109
  (415) 776-5600
  www.buddhistchurchesofamerica.org

Online and Print Resources

- The Dovetail Institute for Interfaith Family Resources
  775 Simon Greenwell Ln.
  Boston, KY 40107
  (800) 530-1596
  www.dovetailinstitute.org

- CrossCurrents
  475 Riverside Drive
  Suite 1945
  New York, NY 10115
  (212) 870-2544
  www.crosscurrents.org

- InterfaithFamily
  (welcomes interfaith families while encouraging Jewish choices)
  90 Oak St.
  P.O. Box 428
  Newton Upper Falls, MA 02464
  (617) 581-6860
  www.interfaithfamily.com

Books for Adults

Hawxhurst, Joan. *The Interfaith Family Guidebook: Practical Advice for Jewish and Christian Partners.* Boston, KY: Dovetail Publishing, Inc., 1998.
(I often recommend this book to Christian/Jewish families with young children.)

Crohn, Joel. *Mixed Matches: How to Create Successful Interracial, Interethnic, and Interfaith Relationships.* New York: Ballantine Books, 1995.
(An in-depth exploration of the issues we have touched on here—practicing one religion or two, celebrating the holidays, appreciating cultural differences, and much more)

Berends, Polly Berrien. *Gently Lead: Or How to Teach Your Children about God While Finding Out for Yourself.* New York: Crossroad Publishing Co., 1997.
(A number of simple, doable suggestions for introducing the concept of God into everyday life and activities.)

Fitzpatrick, Jean Grasso. *Something More: Nurturing Your Child's Spiritual Growth.* New York: Penguin, 1991.
(Good ideas—nondogmatic—on how to help your child connect to the transcendent wonders of the world.)

Kushner, Harold S. *When Children Ask About God: A Guide for Parents Who Don't Always Have All the Answers.* New York: Schocken Books, 1995.
(Some suggested loving answers to the tough questions your child may have, such as, "Who made God?")

Books for Children

Wood, Douglas. *Old Turtle.* Illustrated by Cheng-Khee Chee. New York: Scholastic Press, 2007.
(My all-time favorite children's book, with a subtle but powerful message of tolerance and unity. A lovely gift for a child's baby blessing, to be read to the youngster in years to come by mom or dad or grandparent.)

Ajmera, Maya, Cynthia Pon, and Magda Nakassis. *Faith*. Watertown, MA: Charlesbridge Publishing, 2009.
(An exploration of the many faiths in the world, with wonderful photos showing children participating in various religious practices. *The Global Fund for Children* receives a portion of the proceeds generated from this book.)

Permissions
Acknowledgments

*In the pages of *Bless This Child*, we have culled from a variety of sources. These sources include books, scholarly materials, religious institutions, personal conversations, the Internet, and materials presented to me by the young families who I have served. We have made every effort to identify the selections we offered, including retaining the services of a professional permissions company. If we have inadvertently used material incorrectly or without proper acknowledgment, we apologize. Please do let us know if you have information that will add to our understanding of the sources or the rich history of these inspirational passages. We thank you, in advance, and we will make any appropriate changes or additions in future editions of *Bless This Child*.

About the Author

Susanna Stefanachi Macomb is an ordained interfaith minister. Her extraordinary ceremonies have earned her numerous referrals and features as an expert source in such magazines and newspapers as *New York Magazine, New York Times, Los Angeles Times, Reader's Digest,* the *Associated Press, Time Out, Modern Bride, Bridal Guide, Elegant Bride, Martha Stewart Weddings,* the *Dallas Morning News,* the *South Florida Sun Times, Pregnancy Magazine, Publishers Weekly, Dovetail Journal, AIMS Magazine,* and *San Diego Union-Tribune.* She has appeared on national and local television and radio and is in demand as a speaker at commercial conventions and educational forums. She has been featured in articles for *ABC News, CNN,* and *MSNBC.* She is the author of *Joining Hands and Hearts: Interfaith, Intercultural Wedding Celebrations* (Fireside, 2003), which included the *first* compilation of the major fourteen religious traditions and their tenets of belief, and an extensive menu of readings and rituals appropriate for wedding ceremonies. She lives in New York City with her husband and son.

Susanna is also an artist. Her paintings have been exhibited at Union Theological Seminary and other spiritual and cultural centers.

Andrea Thompson is a New York–based freelance writer and editor.

Made in the USA
Las Vegas, NV
05 November 2021

33766700R00100